I0469804

CONTENTS

 **ntroduction**

The philosophy of success

"It is literally true that you can succeed best and quickly by helping others to succeed."

- Napoleon Hill

You can create many opportunities yourself. You can create these opportunities, for yourself, and for others, by what you know, or find out (research, may be through interview or review). According to Angela Booth, author and writer:

"Business intelligence is always power."

Turning your practice into business requires both creative imagination and intelligence in your field of interest.

Opportunity to develop great business is everywhere. What business can you do RIGHT NOW?

You may or may not have all it takes, but you can develop the necessary skill and experience as you move along.

You can develop the competency through training and education. According to Jim Rohn, American foremost business Philosopher:

"Formal education can make you a living; self-education will make you a fortune."

Give yourself permission to proper. Understand that the more value you contribute the more you will earn if you put yourself in a position to do.

The lesson is simple. You don't have to be an entrepreneur to add more value. But what you must do every day is to continuously expand your knowledge, skills, and your ability to give more.

The aim of this work to go with you on a journey to help you discover and put into action the behaviours you need to create your own great fortune.

You'll be asking who am I and why should you listen to me? To answer the first part of the question is simple. I enjoy helping others reach their potential. I have been writing article in www.Hubpages.com, under the pseudo name "lemmyc" on topics around empowerment, success principles and leadership. In one of my articles **"Money making Ideas: How to turn your passion into profit"-** a reader left these comments:

Cat from romania 14 months ago

very nice of you for offering advice without charging for it :-)

i have a question: i am passionate about helping others (people&animals&plants, etc) I would also need some retirement money, HOW YOU THINK I COULD COMBINE THEM into a business ? In Romania ? pls write to **ondine1960@gmail.com**

thanks

You can read the article through this link:

http://lemmyc.hubpages.com/hub/Money-making-Ideas-How-to-turn-your-passion-into-profit

The comment moved me with compassion and empathy that I had to research so as to organise the information she needed to meet her need. Hence this work is for her, and a host of others who will find the content of this work useful.

I have to point out from the onset that the word fortune is subjective. For one person a fortune could be path to great discovery of wealth and fame, but for another it could as simple as discovering how to turn a specialist knowledge to profit (cash). Either way the knowledge you will discover in this program will put you in good stead on how to turn your knowledge to profit in the bid to creating income streams.

Reading and knowing these principles isn't enough you must take massive action in the bid to turn your dream into a reality.

"We often miss opportunity because it's dressed in overalls and looks like work." - Thomas A. Edison

CHAPTER 1

Windows of opportunity – it's every where
Opportunity – problem or challenge

"Greatness starts by saying yes to an opportunity."

- Mike Litman

"No great man ever complains of want of opportunities."

- Ralph Waldo Emerson

We hear people say that opportunity is everywhere. But what is opportunity? Can we recognise it when we see it? And what do we do with it when we see it?

Opportunity could mean your greatest skill, talent, knowledge or position to contribute by way of providing immediate solution to people's arching needs /want/problem. The ability to provide creative solutions to people's needs in terms of services or products of value is key to a productive life.

Businesses that solve needs win. Businesses that provide value win. Businesses that solve problems win profit.

If your aim as an individual is to put yourself in a position to contribute in a meaningful way as a producer; you need to surrender to your selfishness and address the selfishness of others. Hence you need to pursue opportunities in form of needs, problems, pain points, service, deficiencies and emotions.

There are opportunities to tap into in your areas of expertise. In looking for opportunities you need to seek for the benefit.

In a nutshell opportunity is a solution to an inconvenience or problem. Opportunity is feeling. Opportunity is comfort. Opportunity is fixing pain. The list is endless but more than anything opportunity is an idea.

Perhaps this quote will give you insight on how to recognise or relate with opportunity. When one of the world's greatest investor John Templeton was asked why he was very successful in his choice of stocks.

He said; "My ability to evaluate the true value of an investment."

This is fundamental to creating, recognising and relating with opportunities all around us; since reference shape our belief and value.

I'll leave you with this great quote from William Shakespeare:

"There is a tide in the affairs of men,

Which taken at the flood, lands on to fortune;

Omitted, all the voyage of their life is bound in shallows and miseries."

Competence

"Consciousness or awareness is the source of ability. Learn to become increasingly conscious."

-   *Lao Tzu*

According to the business.com competence have been defined as follows:

1.

A cluster of related abilities, commitments, knowledge, and skills that enable a person (or an organization) to act effectively in a job or situation.

Competence indicates sufficiency of knowledge and skills that enable someone to act in a wide variety of situations. Because each level of responsibility has its own requirements, competence can occur in any period of a person's life or at any stage of his or her career.

2. Law: The capacity of a person to understand a situation and to act reasonably. Disputes regarding the competence of an individual are settled by a judge and not by a professional (such as a doctor or a psychiatrist) although the judge may seek expert opinion before delivering at a judgment; also called legal capacity.

From the above definition it's clear that competence is consists of the knowledge, skills, ability, and personal traits that qualify you to perform a particular task towards achieving the results you need. It provides you with the audacity to compete in the marketplace.

You can develop competence through specialist training and education in your own chosen field. Being competent gives you the impetus to be more creative and innovative in the way you strategize towards achieving your bottom line.

Ultimately it puts you in a position to be an expert and the opportunity to meaningfully contribute to meeting particular need – solve problem or turn resources to instrument for meaningful contribution.

"In order to know a skill exists, it must be named;

In order to develop a skill, it must be practiced.

In order to master a skill, it must be transferred."

- *Anonymous*

"Competencies are the skills, knowledge and behaviours that lead to successful performance."

Commitment

"Memorize and follow the never-fail recipe, get started. Don't quit."
- *Barbara Winter*

There is a great different between interest and commitment. To be committed in any endeavour you have the mind-set of a game player who is determined to win by taking progressive and determined action at every step of the game.

To be committed stipulates that you need to have a clear idea of the decisions you'll make to make you your dream come true. What are you going to do **now**? You need to have a strategy and tactics as well as accountability partners to commit to the fulfilment of your dream.

Moreover, you need to be flexible, creative and innovative in the way you progress towards your determination to realise your dream.

W. H. Murray, an explorer captures the idea of being committed in this quote:

"Until one is committed, there is hesitancy, the chance to draw back, always ineffective concerning all acts of initiation (and creation), there is one elementary truth, the ignorance of which kills countless ideas and splendid plans: that the moment one definitely commits oneself, then providence moves too. A whole stream of events issues from decision, raising in one's favour all manners of unforeseen incidents, meetings and material assistance, which no man would have dreamt would have come in his way."

Until a decision is made, there is no commitment. To become committed is a resolve to do whatever it takes to get the results you require. It is the desire to get result as opposed to reason; and the determination to forge ahead even in the face of failure and uncertainties.

Perhaps this quote, from Kenneth Blanchard, sums up the true meaning of commitment.

"There is a difference between interest and commitment. When you're interested in doing something, you do it only when it's convenient. When you're committed to something, you accept no excuses, only results."

What is your commitment to contributing and winning in this game of life?

You have to realise that all human activities are based on the desire for increase; people are seeking for more food, more clothes, better shelter, more luxury, more beauty, more knowledge, more pleasure ---; increase in something, more life. These are all based on fulfilling the various categories of needs as depicted in Maslow's hierarchy of needs. You will be rewarded for your commitment to using your greatest skills and talents to create products and services to meet these needs. This is summed of in the words of Jones of Toledo; "what I want for myself, I want for everybody."

The Principle of Purpose

"Until thought is linked with purpose there is no intelligent accomplishment."

- *James Allen*

There is a rule or principle that everything in life revolves around. As God's creature you are created for a purpose. There is a reason for your life. What do I mean by this? Well, what is one thing that deep down in your heart, you feel you are here to accomplish. It may not be what you are doing at the moment. But intuitively, you feel that if money wasn't a factor you could spend your life doing this one single thing. You feel very excited, have a great sense of accomplishment, enthusiastic and passionate each time you are doing this activity. Time seems to fly away and you are in a state of flow. Being on purpose is that you develop a laser focused attention to what is important to your life as well as the desire and determination and persistence toward its accomplishment. It's an indication of your passion. Passion is an indication of what you value; it is what holds your attention, and keeps you awake all night long. What do you feel passionate about? Perhaps the following questions will help you in your search.

- What is really important to you in your life?
- What is really important to you in your work?
- What is really important to you in your relationships?
- What would you fight for – defend so long as it's legit?
- Where can you start to make changes?

3 steps to being on purpose

- **Find out what you want to do.**
- **Work out how by achieving your purpose you can serve others.**
- **Look for a way you can combine the two to make money doing what you love.**

The above exercise will help you to find your reason for being – purpose. Purpose brings energy, purpose brings focus, purpose sets you on a pedestal to a new way of thinking, and feeling, and looking for ways to achieve your aims in life. Purpose comes from self-knowledge. You need to think about what your writing reveals about your personal aptitudes and passions.

A simple exercise to define your personal aptitudes and passions

Action

- You need an a pieces of paper to capture your though on the following questions. **What are you naturally good at? What do you perform with ease?**

What is it that you enjoy doing even if it is not the work you do at the movement in terms of your work? The abilities and talents at which you excel are often indicators of where your life purpose lies - especially if you enjoy doing those things

- **What successes have you achieved in relation to the areas associated with your talent?**

What things do you consider to be your greatest successes? May be you are good at encouraging others to realise their potential. You might have an aptitude for making sensible decisions, or have the knack in improving sales and marketing to enable companies to be more productive and profitable.

Whatever you have attained write down:

1. How did it benefit others – for example, feature, advantage and benefit they received.
2. How did it make you feel?

- Is there a cause that you feel passionate about?

Is there something that holds your attention because you care deeply about it? Could your life purpose be based around it? Write you answer down because this could hold the key to defining your purpose in life.

Source: Adapted from Frances Coombes (2008), Self-Motivation. Teach yourself, p.81 with some modifications.

A simple lesson on a life of purpose for you to purse and ponder!

… Henry Ford held unto his dream

…Ford's dream became a reality

…Ford's asset had been his dream and his willingness to devote himself to it.

What is your dream, your reality, and how willing are you to devote yourself to it to making it a come true?

CHAPTER 2

The World of Work (T-WOW) – Value creation factory

"The thoughts of the diligent lead only to plenteousness; but of every one that is hastily only to want."

- *Proverbs 21.5*

"...Autonomy, complexity and a connection *between effort and reward – are most people agree the three qualities that work has to have if it is to be satisfying."*

- Malcolm Gladwell, Author Success Outliers

Work that fulfils those three criteria is said to be meaningful. The work should give us the opportunity to work hard enough and assert ourself (use our abilities – God given gift and talents), and using your mind and imagination, you can shape the world to your desires.

According to Michael Lyatt, in his blog article: "3 Components of Job Satisfaction" for you to have satisfaction in a job you must fulfil three criteria:

1. You must be passionate

2. You must be competent

3. You must create a market

He further analyse these criteria thus:

- Passion + Competence – Market = Hobby

- Passion + Market – Competence = Failure

- Competence + Market – Passion = Boredom

From the above it's clear that any person can create a fulfilling, meaningful and satisfying work by following the above three criteria.

What are you passionate about?

"It's great to find something you love to do and figure out a way to make money from it."

- *Andrew Reynold, Entrepreneur*

Yours passion can come from what you do in your present work or from the things you do in your pastimes. Your pastimes could be any of the following:

Hobbies – activities you do yourself

Leisure pursuits – are activities you watch others do

Voluntary work – activities you do with other people

Your passion could reflect your work commitment to suit your skills and need; as categories by Holland (1973) into the following 6 types:

---

1. **Realistic:** The realistic person seeks objective concrete goals and tasks and likes to manipulate things – tools, machines, animals and

people. They are best suited by agriculture, outdoor, conservation work and similar practical jobs.

2. **Intellectual:** Ideas, words, and symbols are important to this people who are best suited to tasks requiring abstract and creative abilities, suggesting science, teaching and writing.

3. **Social:** These people are best known for interpersonal skills and interest in other people. Social work and counselling are possible career and so is the organising of others.

4. **Convectional:** The convectional person copes with life by following the rules and selecting goals approves of by the big society and customer. Accounting, office work, and administration often suit them well.

5. **Enterprising:** High energy, enthusiastic, dominance, and impulsiveness are the hallmark of thee people, leading to occupations such as sales, politics, entrepreneurial, business or Foreign Service.

6. **Artistic:** The artistic person uses feelings, intuition and imagination to created firms and products, leading most obviously to performing arts, or writing, painting and music.

Source: Holland: Making Vocational Choices, 1973.

Are you competent on this passion of yours or can you acquire competence through training? Can you delegate others to fulfil this expertise?

Can you create a market so as to sell the outcome of your creation?

The key idea here for you is to understand that what you have in your life is the size of your imagination and the level of your commitment to make it a reality. You and you alone have the capability to creating your own **fortune mountain** from your work life. You need to find a Hungary Market.

- Who needs /desires it and why
- Find a new technology for solving the core desire / need
- Find a new way to market this core desire / need to the hungry market (market place).

Dynamics of work and work environment

"Work –it's like a conveyor belt going past with all those packages wrapped up as presents. And I have to tear the wrappings off as quickly as possible to see what's inside and makes sure that nothing gets away."
- Wendy Sullivan of Discovery Works

If you focus your attention on any line of work or occupation, there are two key things that stand out. There is an objective or purpose to satisfy in form of a problem. And there is a customer, client of market place to satisfy. There could be other categories of needs to be met, but in the long run most line of work exists to solve a problem or provide solution to the overarching need/want of the customer. In doing that, they need to satisfy the customer need if the work is to remain productive and profitable.

Are you working in any capacity? What do you do? And what is the outcome of your work – the value you create for your customer? This is in a nutshell the real essence of work; using your greatest skill, talent, gift, knowledge and experience to make a difference in other people's life. Your work will always involve the application of your transferable skills and time to create products or services that benefit your customers. Hence, it could improve you working with people, money/finance, systems, thinking, or involvement in training/learning. Either way, in performing your work you need to be seen as a problem solver. In the performance of your work you need to demonstrate how you have used your skill to make a genuine contribution in term of intangible/tangible outcomes. For example, what you did, made, suggested, improved, showed, tried and changed. How you describe what you've done or what you can do – will make a huge difference to how you are perceived, your attitudes, and even your whole attitude to work. Therefore in the work environment you need to continuously fan and develop these ten generic skills which you will profit from diverse work environments.

10 generic transferable skills for work

- Communication
- Interpersonal skills
- Time management
- Problem solving
- Creativity and Innovation

- Motivation

- Initiative

- Analytical skills

- Flexibility

- Negotiation

If you master these 10 generic skills and be able to demonstrate them in real life situation to solve problems, then you will go a long way prospering in the world of work and beyond.

Why do you work?

The question why evokes lot of meaning to any given situation, circumstance or purpose. If you are asked why you work, it'll evoke a lot of meaning and will challenge you to search your inner most reason or motive as to why you work. This question also deconstructs the link or relationship between value, belief and work. Understanding this concept or idea is the key to living a richer and wealthier life.

For the time being let us focus on the relevance of value to work.

Values are the principles which drive our behaviour; they give meaning to our lives. When we engage in what we do with our values then we engage in projects with our hearts and minds. As mentioned earlier, there is link between belief and value. Our beliefs and values **define** who we are and what we do. In another way, our identity and behaviour determine your destiny.

Your beliefs and values determine the personal rules on which you live.

Values are what make us the way we are, they drive us and provide motivation to how we live our life. Knowledge of our values and awareness of the behaviour that springs from holding such values put us in a position to set clearer goals and make decisions about what's important to us and what we want in life. Values hold the key to living a motivational, successful and rewarding life.

Exercise

Table 2.1 List of common values

Acceptance	Appreciation	Commitment	Cooperation
Accountability	Authenticity	Community	Courage
Accuracy	Autonomy	Compassion	Creativity
Achievement	Balance	Competition	Curiosity
Acknowledgement	Boldness	Comradeship	Democracy
Adaptability	Calmness	Contribution	Dependability
Adventure	Collaboration	Control	Detached
Determination	Harmony	Modesty	Safety
Directness	Health	Morality	Self-awareness
Discipline	Helpfulness	Obedience	Self-reliance
Economic security	Honesty	Openness	Self-respect
Education	Honour	Optimism	Sensitivity
Effort	Humility	Order	Sharing
Elegance	Humour	Organisation	Sincerity
Empathy	Imagination	Patience	Spirituality
Empowerment	Independence	Partnership	Stability

Enthusiasm	Individualism	Peace	Success
Equality	Influence	Perfection	Tact
Excellence	Integrity	Perseverance	Tenacity
Fairness	Intuition	Personal development	Thoughtfulness
Family	Joy	Pleasure	Tolerance
Focus	Justice	Power	Tradition
Forgiveness	Kindness	Prudence	Trust
Freedom	Learning	Quality	Truthfulness
Friendliness	Levity	Recognition	Understanding
Fun	Love	Respect	Variety
Generosity	Loyalty	Responsibility	Vitality
Gentleness	Mercy	Risk-taking	Wealth
Happiness	Moderation		Wisdom

Source: Vickers, A, Bavister, S, Smith, J (2009): Personal Impact –what it takes to make a difference. Prentice Hall LIFE, Harlow, UK. Pp. 30-31.

Look at these values and pick out 5 -10 that you think matters – are important to you or completely describes your tastes.

You can research or find alternate values that you could add to the above.

Next to each list of value that you've selected write a short description of why the value is important to you.

For example if you choose, "Love – it reminds me the very nature of God and having this nature would help me to relate better with God and my fellow men."

Reasons why we work

"One of the most important things about work is to have a passion for what you do."
- *Brad Sugars, Entrepreneur*

The reason (s) why people work could be many and varied. But for the scope of this work I have to narrow it down to just four. I hope that these reasons will help to throw more light as to why people are motivated to work.

Money

As a source to provide for your livelihood and maintain your self –esteem the role of money in the society is evident. Money is a means to transfer or distribute value from person to person. Money – having it or not, has been source of most happiness or unhappiness within the society.

Affiliation

People through work provisions form great team and associates. These associations or affiliation may be in form of support networks for meeting the organisations arching needs. With recent changes in the way we work as well as the way information is organised, there are a lot of these affiliation through social networking sites – Facebook, Google, Hubpages, Yahoo etc,

Meaning

Work gives us a sense of purpose and therefore meaning. Most of the time our passion becomes our work, which ultimately becomes our purpose or mission. To do the work we are passionate about using our

God's given gifts and talents gives meaning and sense of purpose to our lives.

Meet the customer (s) needs – solve a problem

Work gives us the opportunity to become contributors by using our gifts and talents to meet other people problems. It gives us great satisfaction both materially and emotionally in terms of the rewards we get from our customers.

What are your reasons (s) for going to work, and decide which ones are most important to you?

Are these reasons in line with your life's purpose, values, belief and passion?

CHAPTER 3

Entrepreneurial Core Skills – innovative licence to great wealth and prosperity

"High impact entrepreneurs, according to the 2011 High-Impact Entrepreneurship Global Report, are the 4% entrepreneurs responsible for 40% of the total jobs generated by all entrepreneurs."
- *Mauritz Bekker- from the article; How to develop High-impact Entrepreneurs*

Who are entrepreneurs? And what do they do?

It is important to look into the meaning of the word Entrepreneur. Entrepreneur stems from the French words "entre" and "prendre" together which means "do."

Brad Rosser an Entrepreneur bore credence to this say by the time he left Virgin to start his own business.

"...By the time I left Virgin to start up business on my own, I'd had a pretty good training on how to be an entrepreneur. What was most important thing I did learned? That it's not rocket science. There's a lot of chance involved in becoming an entrepreneur, a lot of opportunity. But what marks the entrepreneurs out is that they take these opportunities, rather than thinking of all the reasons why they won't work. It's the different between theory and practice."

Back in 1803 Jean –Baptiste Say (French Economics and Businessman), defined an entrepreneur as "an economic agent who unites all means of production – land of one and labour of another and the capital yet of another and thus produces a product."

There are many definitions of entrepreneur, but the one that makes the meaning clear for a lay man is for me the one described by T. Harv Eker, the author of "Secrets of the Millionaire Mind." He described the entrepreneur as a person who solves problem at a profit. Hence, if you want to become an entrepreneur, you need to become a "problem solver."

Do you want to become a problem solver and be rewarded for meeting the needs of the people you solve their problems? The more people you can solve their problem for profit the more your reward.

It's as simple as that!

Imagine how your life will change if you help many people meet their overarching need through your ability to create effective solutions to their problems by way of products, services or new businesses. Essentially, to become an entrepreneur is to become innovative in the way you do things.

You can read an article "50 Reasons to own your own Business and Celebrate being an Entrepreneur" written by Natalie Sisson – Founder Suitcase entrepreneur by following this link:

http://bit.ly/16kZKO6

What does it then take to become entrepreneur?

I want to make mention of two things that each business or enterprise do in other to exist. One is that they solve a problem and the other thing they do is that they satisfy customer(s). These two points sound a bit simplistic but that in a nutshell underpins the framework under which businesses exist. The entrepreneur needs to understand these key roles in the bid to create a business.

The sole aim of a business is to serve a customer. You serve the customer by helping them to meet their need, and you do it with your best use of your skills and talent.

Skills are the things you need to be able to have the job done. In taking stock – analyses of your skill set, it is important to mention here three types of skill you need to navigate the world of work. These skills are called transferable or functional skills. In the world of work you need to continually re-invent yourself so as to become more proficient in their use. They make you mobile in the world of work. These skills are as follows:

- What you can do with people (interpersonal and communication skills)

- What you can do with information or data (cognitive skills)

- What you can do with objects/things (technical skills)

The skills you need in the world of work are listed below. Perhaps it will be right for you to make a skills audit.

Table 3.1: Skill set evaluation

Evaluating you peoples skills	Evaluating your manual /practical skills	Evaluating your communication skills
Listening to others	**Making repairs**	**Using telephone**
Encouraging other	**Building**	**Dealing assertively**
Resolving conflict	**Taking**	**with people**
Motivating people	**measurement**	**Story telling**
Teaching/Training	**Maintaining**	**Talking to people in**
others	**equipment**	**authority with**
Organising people	**Operating**	**confidence**
Any other	**machinery**	**Writing letters**
	Using a computer	**Completing forms**
	Any other	**Any other**
Evaluating your mathematical /mental skills	Assessing your problem solving skills	Evaluating your creative skills
Memorising figures	Working out routes	Creative writing
Estimating	Crosswords	Designing / decorating a
Planning	Coming up with new	room
Making rapid	ideas	Finding alternative use
calculations	Analysing alternatives	of things
Judging distances	Diagnosing faults and	Craft making
Budgeting	causes of problems	Musical
Keeping accounts	Interpreting data	Drama
Any other	Any other	Improvising
		Cooking
		Using colours creatively
		Any others

You need to personally evaluate you own skills set and create a framework of the following:

Who can I serve by using these skills?

Here I am interested in the field of work or niche that you can use it.

What can I do with these skills in terms of products or services you can develop? Here I am keen on the problem (s) you can solve to your audience by using this skills. If you need inspiration for this task you to refer to Maslow's hierarchy of need.

How can you make this dream come true?

Here I am keen on strategies and tactics and implementation techniques to get the results you earnestly desire.

Exploring the entrepreneurial core skills

In the previous section we've tried to figure out who entrepreneurs are and also what they do. It will be good to explore some of the skills or attributes of entrepreneurs so as to motivate us on how to develop these attributes. For one thing the entrepreneurs "do." Hence it is safe to say that they have a can do attitude. Let us see according to Douglas Cartwright what these attribute look like.

- Have a belief about what is important in life (values).
- Forming those beliefs and values into a relatively coherent vision and purpose.

- Dealing with fear and loss.

- Learning to take risks.

- Developing an optimistic thinking style.

- Taking action

For me these six point or principles summarises the mind-set, skill set and personality traits of entrepreneurs in different fields as they do what they do best – creating opportunities that impact life. For one thing entrepreneurs come in different shades they are contributors, creators, distributors, philanthropists and investors who adopt vehicular mechanisms (resources), by way of technology and human association (great teams) to enable their ideas to become a reality. In a nutshell the entrepreneurs have found ways to take hidden values – idea, information, systems and organise them in a way that would enable people to use them. As they add value they began to create tremendous economic empires. Entrepreneurs throughout history from Sam Walton of the Wal-Mart supermarket to Bill Gates of the Microsoft Fame practice economic alchemy. They are builders and visionaries who create with great imagination and execute excellently.

Core attributes of entrepreneurs

What are the attributes, characteristics, mind set and skill set of entrepreneurs? For us to begin to look at this it's important to first find out what entrepreneurs do. They solve problems for profit. In so doing they create value. The values that they create are two folds:

- They create new products, services and different opportunities.
- The products they create avenues for employment.

Essentially entrepreneurs see opportunities where others see problems and they are able to see emerging patterns in their areas of expertise.

In this section we have to mention some of the core attributes of entrepreneurs. The list is not exhaustive and you can add yours

Artists	Creators	Learners
Adventurers	Modellers	Gatherers
Sportsman	Leaders	Problem Solvers
Risk takers	Managers	Marketers/Sellers
Courageous	Organisers	Networkers
Innovators	Executors/Implementers	Team players
Specialist Knowledge	Practical	Passionate
Strategic thinking	Peak performers	Business Acumen
Success Attitude	Intuitive Abilities	Communicators

It is important to mention here that entrepreneurship is necessary to turn raw materials into valuable problem solving products.

Do you see solutions or possibilities in any given situation?

Look around you; is there a problem around your immediate environment that you would like to solve for profit?

CHAPTER 4

Ideas to great fortune

"All achievements, all earned riches, have their beginning in an idea."

- *Napoleon Hill*

People will always have ideas. But having ideas is not enough in itself. One thing is to have an idea and the other thing is the ability to transform an idea into a reality. This skill can be learned – the ability to transmute an intangible thought to a tangible thing – of a material nature. If you look around you, any of the physical things you see began as a thought in the mind of someone.

There is a very important point that I want to make here. And that is in the issue of knowledge. People will normally say that knowledge is power. But knowledge is only a potential. It only becomes power only when and if it is organised into definite plan of action, and developed to a definite end. It requires creativity and innovation. Having an idea is one thing and developing it constructively in order to solve problems in a meaningful way is important.

But before you can you can transmute desire into its monetary equivalent, you will require a specialised knowledge of the service, merchandise, or profession which you intend to offer in return for fortune. According to Napoleon Hill, in his book "Think and Grow Rich," the accumulation of great fortune call from power, and power acquired through highly organised and intelligently directed knowledge.

However, the knowledge does not, necessarily have to be in the possession of the man who accumulates the fortune.

An important attribute that is required in the ingredient mix towards creating your own fortune is imagination. Imagination is one quality needed to combine specialised knowledge with ideas in the form of organised plans designed to yield riches.

More than anything you need focus and action which will bring you results or rewards, financial, emotional or other expectations. Taking persistence and sustained action toward your goal is the key.

In this section, we will be looking into some examples of people who have applied these success principles towards creating great fortune. The idea here is to learn and acquire some of the strategies and tactics that they used.

"I figured there's no shortage of people in the world with ideas – what's in shortage is action."

- *Peter Thompson*

Asa Candler - The making of Coca- Cola

Everything you see around you in terms of an invention, innovation or discovery began in the mind of someone first as an idea.

The making of Coca cola is not an exception. My motivation for sharing this story is for you to see the steps taken from the initiation of an idea to its conception as a tangible material object. In the story you see the role imagination had to play in making the idea come to fruition. This will help you in your own journey towards the realisation of your dream.

Imagination is the power to think in terms of images, words, or things. It is the workshop of the mind. Here the plan is given shape, form, and made ready for action. This faculty of the mind is able to visualise and imagine an idea into action.

To illustrate the dynamic power of imagination to develop an idea it will be of interest here to recount the story of the making of Coca – cola. The formulation of the ingredients that make up what we now have as Coco-cola drink created by a Doctor. As the story goes, he didn't know what to do with the idea, though he realised that it was of great value. He didn't know what to do with it but he took the formulae to a young drug clerk and explained to him the contents. This formula was only an idea to the old doctor but the young drug clerk paid him five hundred dollars for this idea.

What did the young clerk do?

He turned the idea expressed in that formula over to his imagination. He visualised its value. He discovered that the contents of that formula contained all the essential elements to supply people with a cool and refreshing drink that will make them pause and give them a lift. The idea thrilled the drug clerk to formulate a plan, to put the idea of that formula into action.

He wasted no time in creating a plan for the distribution of what has now become a world famous drink. The drug clerk was called Asa Candler. The drink was Coca – cola.

The little piece of paper, with an idea mixed with the imagination of Asa Candler turned into hundreds of billions of dollar as per the present day.

A sequel to the story is that some years later when the Coca – cola Company was well on the road to prosperity, young man worked into Mr Chandler's Office and suggested to him that he had a plan to double the business of the Coca – cola Company.

For the plan he wanted $25,000 from the Board of Directors who agreed on the offer. The plan was short and to the point and could possibly be the shortest plan in history offered to double a company's business

The plan was "Bottle it."

Imagination is the most valuable faculty by all means develop it.

Ideas to great fortune – the creation of business empires
How 4 people turned their ideas to great fortune.

These stories were reported in the Readers Digest issue of November 2007. The articles were based on four people who successfully set up their own business based on their passion. The title of the article in the Reader Digest people section was, "Got a

£1M Idea? Four who've made fortunes from great ideas shows how it's done. For the purpose of this article I'll the outcome of how they pursued their dream in the table below under the sections:

Who

What they did

How they did it

Obstacles on their way and outcome

Lessons learned

Who	What they did	How they did it	Obstacles on their way and how they persevered	Lessons learned
Rachel Lowe, 30. Owns RTL Games; invented the top-selling board game Destination	She invented a game called destination at 19, while working a cabie driver. While driving her taxi an idea came to her. "Red lights miss a turn." She imagined the taxi as a small piece on a board game, with players – taxi drivers – throwing dice to travel a route past famous landmarks. After every shift she thought out a new twist	She sought for funding by entering her idea to an Enterprise Challenge. Her idea won and she was awarded £500 which helped her to produce the game Destination and start her own company RTL Games. She further researched for ideas on how to make	All the big companies such as Hasbro turned down producing the game for her so she launched RTL Games. She sought for funding through the television programme,	She had this to say: I came up against so many hurdles, and so many doors were closed on me. "If you believe in what you're doing, you have to do it yourself." Despite all these the game was on target to sell 15 versions on Christmas, December 2007 – in London, Paris, New York. Hopefully their

		her game stand out. She targeted the tourist and created a local edition of the game to cater for local attractions. Her contact with local tourist organisation in Portsmouth and London helped her to raise £12,000, which was enough for her first print run of 5,000 games. By 2004, Hamleys toy store in London was set to launch her game for Christmas.	Dragon's Den, but failed. Her business nearly went under in January 2005. She was adamant to sell her shares in order to raise some funds for their new overseas editions. According to her, it was a stupid mistake. The editions got delayed, the containers missed the ship and they lost £150,000 in pre orders for Christmas 2005. But she got on her feet again and did an exclusive deal with Debenhams. From her point of view: "it's all experience."	sale for the year will exceed £1 million.

James Murray Wells, 24. Founded Glasses Direct, selling prescription classes online	While in his final year at the University of Bristol, studying English. James realised that his eyes were getting tired and went to the opticians for some reading glasses. The price was £150 – it came to him as a surprise. He reasoned that there was more metal in a teaspoon compared to the prescription glass. He then contacted an optical lab and found out that the pair of glasses cost £7 to make. The retailer was imposing a 2,000 per cent mark-up.	He then started to delve deeper, researching how glasses are made. He worked out that he could sell them for a fraction of the price over the internet and still makes a profit. He made a note on the university notice board to get someone to set up a website for him at the cost of £6 an hour. Three years on, they were had sold 150, 000 pairs of glasses a year, with a turnover of £4 million. By selling glasses from 315 a pair, they reckon they've saved consumers £40 million to date	H then went to optical labs and found one in the north of England willing to supply his company with lenses. They were put under huge pressure ; since there was a witch hunt to find out who supplied them because they were undercutting the industry	"Build a strong team: people who are experts in your filed." It's not necessary to have a business education to build a successful business. What you really need is a great idea and some guts to make it happen. I surrounded myself with best people I could find. Sheer hard work by great people shapes a business much more than luck.
Jonathan Knight, 24. Owns RedRaven Racing; invented top-selling bike braking system	At the age of 16, Jonathan worked in a bike shop in Belfast and bought his first	He went home and spent eight months on his computer, living off a part-time job in a clothes	He took the design to five engineering companies, but they all said: "We	"Believed in your product. If you get knocked off, get" He learnt to live a purposeful life. For example he would come home from work

bicycle. He got interested in downhill racing. He participated in the race at the age of 20 and won the Northern Ireland championship. In June 2003, he went cycling in Switzerland with his friend who had an accident as a result of brake failure and his bike slammed into a tree. He broke his wrist, collarbone, forearm and femur. This accident was a warming shut for him, because he has seen bikers who had similar experience of brake failure as his friend. The phenomenon is called brake fade. For him the challenge was that there

shop, doing research on structural engineering. He developed an attachment he called the Alpine Rotor. It's made from carbon steel and its wave-like profile helps disperse heat to cool the brake.

don't know you. Go away." According to him he was not deterred, he said, "I always believed in myself and my product. So he went into the engineering faculty in Queen's University in Belfast and just walked into the lab and said to the guys there, "What do you think?" They tested it and it turned out to be 255 more effective than kits market competitors. He then applied for every personal loan he could get, found some suppliers and went into production.

and will be thinking! "Right. What are we going to sell tomorrow …next week …in ten years?" He's glad to be one of the few people he knows who really loves what they do. Running a business isn't rocket science – it's just common sense. He knew there was a demand and this could save lives. He learned from his own experience to contact distributors himself and as word spread in the cycling community they soon started calling him. He realised that the down cycling market is very niche, so they're about to launch range of motocross and motorbike rotors. That's a huge industry.

	should be a better system. As a child he has a habit of tinkering. He felt he could devise a better braking system.			
Michael Welch, 29, Founded Black Circles, online tyre retailer and fitter	The first he did when he left school at 15 was fitting tyres in the local garage in Liverpool – and that was his step int o the industry. Within a year he realised the people around him weren't good. They were buying tyres by rote rather than satisfying customer's individual needs. He saw an opportunity to but better quality tyres, with bigger profit margins, direct from suppliers.	He then started a mail-order tyre business by placing ads in local auto magazines; he also set up a website. He was then 17. At first the suppliers gave him a limited line of credit - £50 a week. As long as he paid on time it was I creased. At 19 he was approached by Kwik-Fit to head up their online business. At that time Ford had just bought Kwik-Fit so he flew to Detroit to meet the customer team. During the meeting he kept asking daft question – the ones everyone else was thinking but was	He tried to enrol on Liverpool University's Basic accountancy course but they said he couldn't because he didn't have qualifications. He had one GCSE in English and something like an F in Business studies and an E in maths, but he kept asking the vice principal until he agreed. They had him in for an assessment and saw that the business had grown and let him on to the degree	"Be honest and give value for money. Put the customer first." Listen to what Michael had to say about their sales strategy and the effectiveness of their business model "Seventy –five per cent of our sales are from repeat or referred customers." "We stay ahead by doing what we do better than anyone

		embarrassed to ask. To his surprise everyone toed the party line rather than challenging it. He like being in control and after a year he left with a month's salary and started the Black Circles. In six years their revenue has reached £10 million. Customers order tyres over the internet and get them fitted within a day at one of 900 affiliated garages.	course.	else."

Having read through these experiences of these four entrepreneurs, what are the take away in terms of their vision, discipline, passion and attitude towards their accomplishments?

"A blind man's world is bounded by the limits of his touch; an ignorant man's world by the limits of his knowledge; a great man's world by the limits of his vision."

-E Paul Harvey

If your vision –your dream is great, then so is your potential for success.

CHAPTER 5

Idea and idea conception

An idea is our visual reaction to something seen - in real life, in our memory, in our imagination, in our dreams." ~ Anna Held Audette from the book, The Blank Canvas

Take some time now, and look around you. You must have realised that everything – articles or objects all around you were at one time an idea in one's mind. It was invisible at one time and over time through the creative ability given to man by God it was made visible. Even at this point in time you might have an idea concerning something. But any idea without practical action to its accomplishment or achievement is just a notion.

An idea is an image formed in the mind. It is a mental picture of something seen, heard, or thought; the formation of a pattern by which something is developed or created.

From the above definition some words do stand out – **image, mind, mental picture, and pattern, developed or created**. On the whole the idea could be applied to immediate raw materials in our environment – data, things, or people.

Valuable ideas when developed and implemented to the service of man could be a source to great wealth. In his book Applied Psychology: Driving Power of Thought, Waren Hilton wrote the following about ideas:

As Mr. Waldo P. Warren says, "Who can measure the value of an idea?" Starting as the bud of an acorn, it becomes at last a forest of mighty oaks; or beginning as a spark it consumes the rubbish of centuries.

"Ideas are as essential to progress as a hub to a wheel, for they form the center around which all things revolve. Ideas begin great enterprises, and the workers of all lands do their bidding. Ideas govern the governors, rule the rulers, and manage the managers of all nations and industries.

Ideas are the motive power which turns the tireless wheels of toil.

Ideas raise the ploughboy to president, and constitute the primal element of the success of men and nations.

Ideas form the fire that lights the torch of progress, leading on the centuries.

Ideas are the keys which open the storehouses of possibility.

Ideas are the passports to the realms of great achievement.

Ideas are the touch-buttons which connect the currents of energy with the wheels of history. Ideas determine the bounds, break the limits, move on the goal, and waken latent capacity to successive sunrises of better days."

Why am I writing this article? Well. I believe like me you have been in the time past or now in a position where you had a great idea, but do not know how to transform the intangible idea to a tangible form of material form. I want you to join me in this journey where we will explore the working of the human mind and the development of ideas through the organisation of specialist knowledge.

By specialist knowledge I mean that knowledge you need to make your ideas a reality by organising it to a particular end – for example, the creation of riches or wealth.

It is important to point out that riches are the material realisation of financial imagination. On the other hand, the wealth of the world is but the sum total of the contribution of the creative thoughts of the successful people of all ages. This creative ability is not limited to a particular individual or professions. Through training and exercising of your mental acuities you can learn to develop imagination faculties so as to reap the rewards thereof. Understanding the basic lessons in idea creation and idea selling is the key to unlocking your imagination. This work will guide of working with ideas intelligently to create abundance.

Players in the idea marketplace

"We get paid for bringing value to the market place."

- *Jim Rohn*

Essentially, there are three players in the idea marketplace. They are the idea producers the idea distributors and the idea consumers. In the article "The Idea marketplace" the various players in the market place are grouped as follows.

Idea producers	Idea Distributors	Idea Consumers
Scientists	Schools	All others
Writers	Television	
Inventors	Books	
Engineers	Religion	
Politicians	Individuals	

There are two ways to become a player that can use his/her imagination for creating a fortune or to affect the life of others.

One is to dream and be willing to take action on your dream and make it a reality. The other is to manifest the thought you have in your creative imagination, explore options and act to make them real by conscious creation of reality.

In this article the idea is to encourage you to become a person that is able to create and put your ideas into work. You have the tools and equipment you need to do this from birth. All you need is to become attentive and aware of it. Doing it however, is not instinctive; you have to invest in yourself to learn the skills. The ideas here could be the beginning for you. Listen to what Robert G Allen – The Best Selling of Multiple Income Streams said about you and your value:

"What I want you to realize is that you, your life story or your life's expertise have market value. It may have enough market value to support you for life."

CHAPTER 6

Idea and Imagination in harmony with specialised knowledge

How to turn idea to cash – Earl Prevette Experience

And what you can learn from it!

"Ideas are inexhaustible, they are limitless. Capture one, adopt it, create a body for it, and make a real child of it, the child sometimes grows to a giant."

- Earle Prevette

One of the often neglected principles of any business is selling. Without selling there is no means of generation income or profit in form of cash.

Most of the time your sell your, idea, talent or skills, your products or service or other people's products or service packaged one form or another.

Ultimately, you sell something of value in exchange for your contribution to serving others.

The aim of this article is to describe the steps taken by Earle Prevette as described in his book which he a simple idea of life insurance and earned millions of dollars in profits as a result. The article is to inspire and motivate like minds interested in how to transmute ideas of any sort to profit.

The selling process likened to farming

"We are going to be like farmers. We are going to plant seeds, and these seeds that we plant are the seeds we're going to reap."

John E. Shoaff , One of American foremost Entrepreneur

Selling could be likened to farming. In farming, the farmer has to plant the seed, in doing so; he has an assurance of a crop. He does know that he must *sow* before he can reap. From the Scriptures, we learn that "whatsoever ye sow, that ye shall reap." The Mosaic Law tells that everything in nature increaseth after its own kind. Simply this is the principle of cause and effect.

The farmer is likened to the salesman. The farmer plants the seed. The salesman plants ides of hid sale. The idea of your product; seed, will never grow a crop of sales unless they are planted. The salesman reaps as he sows –"the seed of idea." The more he sows the more sales he will reap.

The impact of technology on selling

At any stage in human history, technology has really helped men to achieve more than their peers. The wave of technological innovation does help to leverage results to different endeavours; of which sale is one.

According to Earle Prevette, to sell by telephone it was necessary to build ideas around your product. The ideas must convey the VALUE of the product to the prospect. The prospect can only react on ideas. He is a negative force, you are the positive force. Suggestions come from you. Reactions will follow from him – your prospect.

The ideas of your product are seed you plant. The telephone helps you to plant more in a more scientific and systematic way.

In today's environment, how can you use technology, like the internet to sow more seed of your idea?

Building a sales plan – on the idea of life insurance

In his story, Earl Prevette realised that for him to have crop of life insurance sales, he must sow crops of life insurance ideas. He lost no time, in building a SALES PLAN around the idea of life insurance. He building the plan he studied life insurance from every angle not a phase of the subject was overlooked. Indeed, he became an expert. He sought every available source of *knowledge* and *information.* He read every book he could find in the subject; compared all major companies. He realised the important types of polices including the terms insurance, ordinary life, limited payment life, endowments, all forms of annuities, and retirement income plans. He reckoned that motility tables, compound interest tables, life expectancy tables, cash reserves, disability clauses, waivers of premium clauses, and tables for optimal purposes. He searched the tax laws both State and Federal.

In short, the sound economic and financial aspects of life insurance as an institution was carefully weighed and considered. His observation was the institution of life insurance was the steel girder holding together the economic structure of the nation.

After getting saturated with life insurance, he began to study the prospect. Where does he fit in? Where is his place in the great network of economic, social, and financial relations?

He reckoned that the system was set up for one purpose and for one purpose only, and that was the need of the prospect.

From his study he can to this to this verdict: "a life insurance policy was a declaration of financial independence, embodying guarantees that solve the social, economic, and financial problems of the prospect, and make sure that his hopes, ambitions and need are met.

The prospect did not know this (special knowledge); according to Earle, he must tell him.

He then made the prospect the centre of the plan. According to him, he made the prospect the hub of the wheel and the spider in the web. He draped the insurance policy around his shoulder. He idealised the plan to the prospect. He made it talk, visualised and revealed its benefits and what it meant to the both the prospect and his family.

Result of the sales plan

The ideas of the life insurance incorporated into a sales plan in two hundred words put into action by faith become a force. It arrested attention, it incited interest, and it persuaded and convinced the prospect to act. It created sales, it produced results, and it turned the idea of life insurance into money.

CHAPTER 7

Working with ideas – from idea to ideal

In the forgoing sections, we have tried to describe the meaning of idea. But an ideal is a perfect image, and establishes the true conception of the things you want to create or the event you want to bring about in your experience. It is also important to understand the link or relationship between desire and plan. But first we need to know what desire is and what plan is all about.

Desire is possibility seeking expression and, or function seeking performance. Desire is different from wish because desire has a level of passion. To wish for something is more about having a thought about having something. A desire for something has an energy or passion about getting it. In most cases it is has been described as "burning desire." On the other hand an intention is a decision to act to get or manifest what is desired. How is made possible? You need a plan.

Plan

What then is a plan? A plan is a method of action, procedure or arrangement. It is a program to be done. It is a design to give effect to an idea, a thought, a project or the development of something. A plan for example, may ask a simple question: "what do you desire?" May be you desire to sell something, desire a job, desire more clients. Desire to break into a market with new products, the list is endless. Whatever you desire in terms of these questions pertain to present or future occupation or accomplishment. Plan is the way to make your desire known. It conveys to people in plain language a definite concept of what you are offering for consideration. A plan is therefore the principle to scientifically and effectively organise thoughts into a plan. It is important to point out here, that al who made contributions in service, inventions, discoveries and science, have given their idea either a body or a plan. An idea means nothing until it is incorporated into a plan or built into a body.

How to prepare and form an idea for sell: merchandise.

1. Select the idea you want to accomplish
2. Define and enumerate the idea in terms of services, thing or proposition and visualise its values and advantages in concrete terms.
3. Arrange the idea and its advantages in sequence and give it a solid plan or body. Your power to do this by four laws namely:
4. The law of faith

   - Idealise the plan, and see it attracting and getting results. Reinforce

Faith is the substance of things hoped for and evidence of things not seen. The beginning of any great accomplishment is the determination that it will work even before it is manifested. The idea is intangible first. But through the eye of faith you'll see the possibility of the idea being transformed to reality. Faith is a fundamental Biblical principle.

Permit me to add here a very important except from the transcript given by one of the Americans foremost Millionaires John E Shoaff who mentored Jim Rohn, Here it is:

"So, what is success in your life? What is it that you want? Define it. Write it down. Pinpoint every drop of that dream that you have in your mind. Define it so clearly on that piece of paper that you can completely see it in your mind. And when you get it written down, write "thank you" on it and plant that seed and put it away, and it will start to materialize and it will start coming into your life."

According to him this is the law of acceptance that what you want even though you've not received it physically have been delivered. It sets into motion the law of sowing and reaping, law of cause and effect and synergism of the working of the two minds – the conscious and the subconscious. The conscious mind involves and the subconscious evolves.

- The law of repetition

Repetition has been attributed as the "mother of all skills". It's a memory tool that gives you impetus to rehearse and practice your part in a great play or act until it becomes a second nature. The practice of the act of repetition makes any act perfect.

- The law of Imagination

This is the power of visualisation. It is the act of celebrating a great event through a clear cut plan. It's said that imagination is greater than knowledge.

"When you visualize something, this is the thing you are going to bring into your life, if the visualization is strong enough."

- John E Shoaff

- The law of persistence

You need to believe in your plan and with great determination and persistence see it to fruition. This is by following through in your daily, weekly, monthly and yearly task or activities towards the accomplishments of your goals. You also need to work with your accountability partners who are working closely with in one form or the other.

- The law of action

You need to take mass action towards the attainment of the set goals. No matter the idea, plan or process, without positive and determined action your idea or plan will not come to fruition. It is important to realise that the perfection of any business, art or craft is determined by your attitude. The right attitude towards your job taps a hidden reservoir of knowledge and experience and put you in a vantage position to accomplish your goal.

5. Have a plan

According to Peter Drucker, Planning defines the particular place you want to be and how you intend to get there. Planning does not substitute facts for judgement nor science for leadership. It recognises the importance of analysis, courage, experience, and intuition – even hunch. It is responsibility rather than techniques.

Having a plan is important but working your plan is even more important. The plan should not be written in stone. As per the realisation of the plan you need to adopt a flexible stance in term of making it a reality. For example, the some variables in your system and environment as per your former plan can change but you need to always figure out where you are in terms of your plan coming true. Make room for adjustments and be willing and determined to forge ahead based on new light to your former plan.

CHAPTER 8

Develop a creator mentality

"Expect wonderful things. Be a creator of ideas. Let's not be moons, the reflector of ideas. Let's be suns, let's be the creator of the light; let's be the creator of the ideas, because we all have a capacity--that guardian of the gate, as the conscious mind."

- *John E Shoaff*

I sincerely believe that God who created us in His image and after His likeness has put His spirit in us and has given us the ability to create. Just like any gift we need to open it, become hilarious in the possibilities that surround us in our ability to use and enjoy it. Perhaps in the zeal to explore the various dimensions we can choose to exercise this great choice and freedom within us all.

What does it mean to develop a creator mentality? Why do we need to develop it? And how can we develop it? Where and when can we use it?

Maybe describing the benefits of what creators do will spur us into the frenzy of desiring to become one. I read an article by Donald Miller is the founding Director of Storyline, an organization that helps people live better stories - you can see it through this link:

http://storylineblog.com/2011/02/24/three-characteristics-of-a-great-creator

To summarise his thoughts he said that a creator makes things. He went on to list these 3 attributes of a creator to and advice given to him from a friend – Steve Taylor; to which I have added one more idea with modifications.

- A creator loves what loves what they do – **passion/purpose**
- A creator knows how to do what they do – **competence/will to do**
- A creator does what they do – **action and result driven**
- A creator evaluates what they do – **continuous improvement**

The key points from the article are as follows:

- The best way to get discovered is to work very hard, very long hours and get good. People discover what is good. Permit me to include that you can learn from those who have become experts in the field of your endeavour.
- A creator focuses, hoes some land for decades and keeps the soil fertile. He isn't lazy he works every day, moving the plot forward.
- In addition a creator actually makes things happen. Creative talk and exploration is not the same as the act of creation. A creator can hold in their hands what they have made. Little blog entries won't do and poems won't do. A creator makes thing.
- From the fourth point that I've included, it's clear that the creator doesn't glory in past laurels but always evaluates the results to see how best to improve constantly and consistently. This is feedback.

The steps to mental development

Mental strength will always stump physical strength. Well, I can hear you ask; "what do I mean by this statement?" The evidence abound in every area of life – academics, sports, business and any other endeavour that require the development of our mental faculties. Have wondered why a particular football team wins over another. Outwardly they appeared to have given the entire can but the better side worn. What is the secret for them to snatch this victory at the last minute or even second s to the end of the match? It simply boils down to share mental strength. Why do we have to develop mental strength and why is preferred to physical strength? The answer is very simple; every successful outcome doesn't start from the thin air. It is first formed in our imagination and the ability to develop and use the imagination is the key to mental development as well as success in material or physical world. Briefly, I'll discuss steps to mental development.

Steps to mental development

There are three processes to mental development:

1. Getting information from a sense to its associated brain centres which then make the mind centre conscious that particular information has been transmitted to it.
2. Organising the information in the mind centre with relation to other information previously brought to the mind

3. The mind centre directs its co-related brain centre to send out a certain impulse of action to the corresponding muscular structure.

How does this apply to real life?

Let us analyse an illustration of the three process of mental development. Suppose you first heard something that concerns particular prospect for 'goods of sale'

Second you comprehend the significance to you of what you heard.

Third, your mind directs your muscle to make a particular use of what you comprehend.

The original mental impression has been fully developed because you employed all three processes. If you had not completed the cycle of development, you could have given your mind only partial exercise with what you heard.

This ability of developing your mental acuities in order to act to the stimuli impressed in your sense through perception is relevant in your development as an idea seller and therefore a master salesman.

The idea for creating this work was borne out of the request of a customer who read an article I wrote; and asked for more enlightenment on how to develop her interest to business.

The ability to achieve and work on all the three cycles of mental development is fundamental to success and great achievement. Success only comes to the person who acts most effectively on what he knows; after all, you are not paid for what you know but what you do with it now and how you impact other peoples' life with it.

Walter Disney Model of Creativity and Innovation – a motivating example

Who is Walt Disney and why should I bother you with the model of his creativity instincts? Well the answer is simple. Walt Disney had the ability had the ability to connect his innovative creativity with successful business strategy and his expertise in this areas enables him to create an empire in the field of entertainment that had survived decades even after his death. Disney is a symbol of one who had the ability to create a successful company based on creativity. He represents the process of turning fantasies into concrete and tangible expressions. His platform for the expression of his ideas, the animated films, characterizes the process of all creative genius. The ability to take something that exists only in their imagination, and forge it into physical existence that directly influences the experience of others in a positive way is something of great value. Due to this ability of transformation of idea to reality, Disney has built a huge empire that is solely dedicated to amusement and entertainment. Even after so many years since he has gone, his idea is story board created as idea in film making is also being applied in different industries where information need to be organised.

How was Disney able to create this ability in personal creativity and innovation that distinguished him as an important contributor to the entertainment industry?

Through the field of Neuro Linguistic Programming it is possible to study the perceptual maps of people who have had great success in their field with the possibility of modelling them. Disney's strategy of personal creativity revealed that there are three arch types of creativity which are found to exist in Disney. These are Disney, the dreamer, the realist and the critics. Each of these personality types as it relates to creativity has a fundamental during different phases of the creative process.

The attributes of the personalities as well as the table of their various characteristics are described below.

Dreamer: innovation – reformulation of goals.

Realist: implementation/invention – reformulation of operations.

Critic: discovery – reformulation of filters and evidence procedure.

There are four levels or contexts in the Walt Disney's strategy for implementing personal creativity. These levels are:

The focus level, Cognitive style, attitude and basic micro strategy. Each of these four levels is related to the three personalities in the Walt Disney creativity model. Under the level of focus in the dreamer you have (what), for the realist (how), and for the critic (why).

For the cognitive style we have under the dreamer (Vision Big Picture), Realist (Action Short Term Steps), and for the critic (logic Avoiding Problems by finding what is missing).

In the place of attitude, under dreamer (Anything is possible), realist (Act "as if" it is possible), and under critic ("what if" Problems occurs?).

In the Basic Micro Strategy, under Dreamer (Synthesizing the senses), under Realist (Associating into Characters 'Storyboarding') and Critic (taking 'Audience' Perspective).

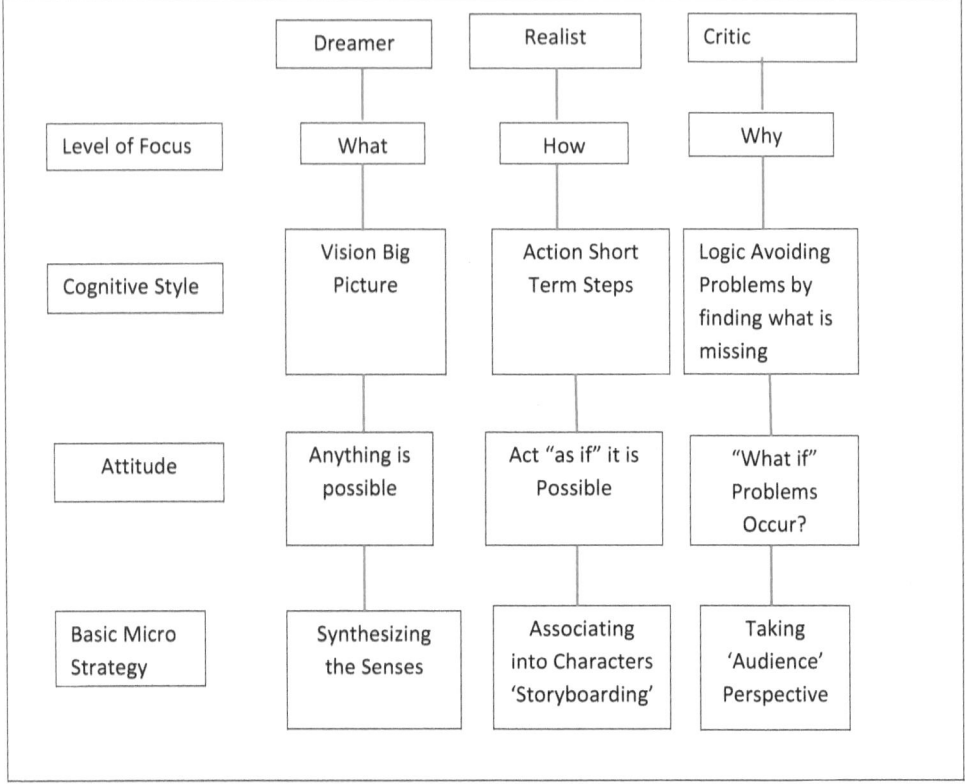

Table 8.1 Walt Disney's Personal Creativity Strategy, taken from, Dilts Robert B. and Gino Bonissone (1993). "Skills for the Future: Managing Creativity and Innovation." Pp.144, Meta Publications Cupertino, California.

Developing these attributes on a personal basis is important to personal creativity and personal leadership. It enables to be able to take initiative, developed your decision making skills as well as creative and innovative abilities. On the whole as you become proficient in these skill sets you will become more creative and productive as well as profit in any idea you desire to develop.

CHAPTER 9

Selling and the selling process

"It is you that you offer for sale. With your traits ranged in like goods in the shelf. And the first thing to do is to make a success of yourself."

- *Edgar .A. Guest*

The Idea Seller - Selling a thought

How do you sell your thought? Well, there is only one way to indicate or express what is going on in your mind. Your thought can be physically shown only by muscular action of some kind. Brain and nerve action are hidden, but muscle action need to be expressed in one form or the other for it to be perceived. If your muscular action expresses exactly the idea you desire and will and use it to manifest your thought another person, then, your idea sold. Therefore you can only make another person conscious of your thought only by some perceptible physical manifestation of the idea you wish to convey him.

Imagine the joy of having the idea creator and idea seller in one person; Or else been able to create a framework to enable such skill mix to be available to you at will. As an idea seller you should be able to answer the following question about your creative endeavour.

1) Do you sell something that clearly solves a problem?

2) Do you have a way of identifying and communicating with your potential customers?

3) Do they have the willingness and ability to pay?

Fulfilment of steps 1 and 2 is not an option; the third premise must be fulfilled for your creation – product, service or merchandise to be worthwhile.

To sell therefore you need to find ...

1)   People who have a problem that you/your product/service can sort... and;

2) Do you have a way of identifying and communicating with... and...

3) Who have the ability/pockets/willingness to pay you to sort out their problem?

Creation of great fortune – the creator of ideas meets the seller of ideas

"Imagination is the beginning of creation. You imagine what you desire you will what you imagine and at last you create what you will."

- *George Bernard Shaw*

In your journey to creating your financial breakthrough you need to arm yourself with the ability of being a great creator of idea – make things and or a seller of idea. You may not need to be a creator of the idea for sale or the idea seller to make your fortune. But at least the making of great fortune in reaches or wealth demands that you need to know how to work in partnership with those that create great value. Howbeit, you can become a distributor of those products or services of value as the case may be.

It's not enough to create a good product or service. You also need to be able to create a formidable sale system to sell and market your product or services to your prospect and clients as the case may be.

The idea here is that developing your competence as a creator and seller of ideas will put you on the road to acquiring great riches. In becoming a creator of ideas you need to become an expert in your own terms – possession of some sort of specialist knowledge. You may not need to be in possession of this knowledge but at least you know how to acquire it.

You need to also develop the expertise you need to sell your idea or you may know where to find this knowledge. The idea of selling is very important.

In her book Successful Selling, Christine Harvey outlined the following benefits of selling:

- opportunities of self – development
- opportunities for promotion
- opportunities for helping other people
- job satisfaction
- financial wealth
- progression towards running your own business

From the foregoing, it's clear that becoming a creator and seller of ideas will put you the best position to realising your dream to a prosperous business life. It doesn't matter the field of your expertise.

Steve Forbes, in his book "A New Birth of Freedom", sums this idea up in these words thus:

"The real source of wealth and capital in this new era is not material things – it is the human mind, the human spirit, the human imagination

and our faith in the future. That's the magic of a free society- everyone can move forward and prosper because wealth comes from within."

Selling Process in 12 steps

"Sales skill is the dynamic factor of success. It transforms potential powers into actual accomplishments. It enables the qualified man to turn his individual capabilities to best account."
Norvan A Hawkins – Author of Uncertain Success

Selling is only single activity that adds cash to your bottom line. You may have all the ideas, knowledge and skills but unless you are able to position yourself to where those who need them will find you, it's of no value to you.

In his book "Certain Success" by Norval, A Hawkins; he reasoned that for an individual to be successful in any market place the following principles must be understood and applied in your particular areas. It is made up of the following four vital steps:

(1) Knowing how to sell

(2) The true idea

(3) Of one's best capabilities

(4) In the right market or field of service.

These four points above is key for you to prospers as an individual in any market – your ability to sell.

Know how to sell

Selling is specialist knowledge. What do I mean by this statement? From my point of view what good is an idea, proposition, information or knowledge if you cannot sale it to others?

The true idea

What is the value of the idea that you want to sell. Of what benefit will it be to your prospects? How will the idea impact their lives as to who they become, what they do and the result they achieve?

Of one's best capabilities

Your capabilities signify the things you are able to do with your gifts, talents, abilities, skills, experience and dispositions (personality traits and aptitudes). You should be able to identify your gift and talent which is what you'll use to create your products, program or services for your area of expertise. The next is to know the right market to sell it.

In the right market or field of service

You make money by selling your product or service, other people's products or services. These endeavours were made possible by transforming your ideas on a particulars area of your expertise to something of value – merchandise.

Become a master salesman

Mastering the art of selling or rather the processes involves in making a sale is important if you are to make great fortune from your idea creation.

The section describes the 12 steps in the selling process.

1. Preparation for selling

2. Prospecting

3. The plan of approach

4. Securing an audience

5. Sizing up the buyer

6. Gaining attention

7. Awakening interest

8. The creation of desire

9. Handling objections

10.   The Process of decision

11.   Obtaining signature of accent

12.   The getaway that leads to future orders

Source: "Certain Success" by Norval, A Hawkins

Preparation for selling

Selling like any business endeavour requires a lot of preparation. It's generally said that if you fail to plan, then, you plan to fail. Preparation before any other thing is an important step to making sale. What then is preparation for sale? How will I make it happen?

Prospecting

Who are your clients, customers or audience? Where are they? And how can they be contacted? Essentially, the key thing is to be aware of how to fish out your prospect (would be customers), and how to make them aware of your products or services.

The plan of approach

If you fail to plan, then you plan to fail. Just like any other accomplish in life, if you desire to sell, then you need to have a plan for sale. This requires intelligence on your part as a seller of ideas.

Securing an audience

You need to have clarity of thought and action about how to target your audience as well as make then develop interest in your idea. What is the unique selling point of your product? How will it improve the life of your audience in terms of the benefits? How do you attract their attention?

Sizing up the buyer

You should be able to understand the market place as well as the segment or niche you need to focus on. Who are your competitors and why should customers buy from you and not from them? Are they able to pay for your product? This is the key to success in your selling ambition. This is true because if they are unable to pay for your product then sale would not happen; and income will not be generated.

Gaining attention

Gaining the attention of your potential prospects or would be customers is very important aspect to gaining attention. In real life, if you want to gain the attention of someone, you need to gain their attention. Gaining attention is a strategic process that you need to use to attract your prospect. It ranges from using attention grabbing headlines to being selective in terms of the platform and medium that you employ to attract your customers.

Awakening interest

This is simply being able to ask yourself this souls searching question in terms of the benefits of your products or service to your customers. Why should they buy from you and not from your competitors? In sales the needs of the customer is paramount and not your product. You should be able to find out what's in it for me (WILFM), in terms of benefits of your product or service.

The creation of desire

How do you create desire to your potential prospects? One key thing about desire is that it's the final state in the mind for you to take action. In the process of copyrighting technique (AIDA), some people include conviction before action. In case you don't know AIDCA, means, attention, interest, decision, conviction and action. What are the things that create desire in the mind of your prospects?

Handling objections

It doesn't matter how you look at it, selling is offering another form of proposition to someone. There is always an obstacle to surmount between the buyer and the seller. You need to persuade the buyer beyond all reasonable doubts that you product or service is of great value; hence will provide the solution to the problem that the buyer is anticipating. Hence there is the issue of credibility, ingenuity and guarantee to the promise that you are making. Some of the ways you could answer to these questions that the buyer has in mind is to put yourself in the position of the buyer. You should be able to provide on the spot answer to these questions.

Why should the customer buy from you and not form your competitors?

What puts you in good stead to provide the solution to their problems?

What can other customers say concerning your product or service?

How will you assure the customer that your offering is of value and that they have the freedom or guarantee to return their goods if they don't like it?

The earlier you can supply the answer to these questions as you communicate your message to the prospects the easier will your sale process be.

The Process of decision

You need to understand the psychology of human behaviour for you to master the process of decision making. The process is three prongs – arouse their attention, keep them interested and bring them to the frame of mind for them to make decision. The words that you use in each stage as well as the way and manner by which the words are crafted are of great essence.

Obtaining signature of accent

What are the ideas you can use to persuade your prospects to believe in you offering beyond reasonable doubt? For example, you can use words from witnesses who have benefited from you service or products. You can also create an artificial scarcity of your idea or product in terms of making your prospects feel that they are losing out if they don't act quickly. You can also create a sense of urgency by giving special privilege to those who act immediately.

The getaway that leads to future orders

On the whole as a master sales man you need to be creative and adaptive to developing products and services to meet the future needs of your prospect. His requires continuously developing valuable products in the back end to carter for the needs of your clients.

CHAPTER 10

Power to take initiative - empowerment

Four human endowments – implications to decisions you make

"Between stimulus and response there is a space. In the space lies freedom and power to choose our response. In that choices lie our growth and happiness."

We've all been blessed with great gifts (all human beings) of freedom and choice. But closely linked and locked in very loose mesh with these two free gifts is the ability to make decision. This power of being also to make decision is the key that unlocks our destiny at any moment in time. However, being able to make decision exposes us to the great law and principle of cause and effect. Every decision we make sets this law into motion. We need to become aware of this great truth which is a guiding light to all we'll ever be, do or achieve.

William Jenning Byrant had these to say about destiny:

"Destiny is not a matter of chance but a matter of choice. It is not a thing to be waited for; it is a thing to be achieved."

The outcome of the above explanations is that we are to be 100% responsible on how we use these four endowments that have been freely given to us. Knowing that they exist is not enough but using them intelligently holds the key to our realising our dreams in different areas of life.

These four natural endowments have been freely given to us. One thing is to realise that we have them. The other thing is to know how to make the best use of these natural endowments that have been freely bestowed on us. From the forgoing, we have the choice and freedom to make decisions. It does require us to have the wisdom to make the right choices which does impact on our belief and values. These decisions have to be of value and also align to our most arching goals that are based on principles.

We'll be discussing these four endowments more in this section.

Self –awareness

This is our capacity to stand apart from ourselves and examine our thinking, our motives, history, our scripts, our actions, and our habits and tendencies. It enables us to put ourselves apart cognitively speaking and evaluate and re-evaluate out precepts and objectives and how we stand in our present environment.

Conscience

It's mentioned somewhere that the man's conscience is the candle of the Lord searching through his hidden motives. Stephen Covey in his book, "First Things First", he wrote that conscience connect us with the wisdom of the ages and the wisdom of the heart. It's like our internal navigational system that points us to the true magnetic north. It gives us a sense of our unique gifts and mission.

Creative imagination

Creative imagination resides in the realms of the imaginative faculty – the human mind; giving us the ability to create. It endows us with the power to envision the future a future state, to create something in our mind, to solve problems harmoniously and synergistically. It enables us to see the preview of an envisioned future and enjoy it even in our mind even before it becomes a reality. In operating in the realm of the creative intelligence we give ourselves permission to align our faculties with finite intelligence to work in harmony with the Divine intelligence. The key thing is that our creative imagination is based on principles of God in the reality we want to bring birth to – create. After all, God is the creator of all things.

Independent will

As a human being you are have an independent will. This has given you the impetus as God's creation to have the freedom to make choices. These freedom and choices are within the remit of you being able to operate with independent will. Independent will is then our capacity to cat. According to Stephen R. Covey in his book, "First Things First", it gives us power to transcend our paradigms, to swim upstream, to rewrite our script, to act based on principles rather than reacting based on emotion or circumstance.

The important point here is for us to realise that this natural endowment of independent will helps us navigate the rigours posed by nature or nurture, in the area of environmental or genetic influences. Though these influences – environmental or genetic may be powerful or limiting, they do not control us. We need to realise that you are neither victims nor products of our past. We are products of our choices. We are "response-able" – able to respond, to choose beyond our moods or tendencies.

In conclusion, the development of each of the four endowments and their working together is the core of personal leadership. Understanding these gives us confidence and sums our thoughts in the words of Stephen Covey as follows:

"I can examine my paradigms. I can examine the results they're producing. I can use my conscience to determine new paths that are in harmony with principles and with my own unique ability to contribute. I can use my independent will to make choices to create change. I can use my creative imagination to create beyond my present reality, to find new alternatives."

I have discussed this aspect of four natural endowments because understanding their use and how they are linked to personal leadership is the key to growth, change and contribution. It requires initiative and the confidence to move into the unknown; an aspect of risk taking. But application of these principles will keep these risks under control as you navigate into the unknown.

CHAPTER 11

Make sense of self and environment

"You can get stronger, you can get wiser, and you can get better. Remember the trio of words: stronger, wiser, better. The winter won't change but you can change."

-Jim Rohn

I have been a student of personal development and have positioned myself to learn from a lot of experts in this field. Your thought is the beginning of everything that you can ever achieve or accomplish in life. Gradually from my experiences you need to develop in two areas – the way you thing and the ability to control and leverage your environment. From the schools of leadership and management palace you do the right things and do the right things right. This idea was echoed in by Stephen R. Covey in his book 'First Things First.' It is leadership before management.

Life is in a constant flux of change. We can only but make sense of the changes around us but in order to do this we need to continuously seek to reinvent ourselves.

James Allen summed this up in his book As a Man Thinketh: "The within is ceaselessly becoming the without."

"From the state of a man's heart proceed the conditions of his life; his thoughts blossom into deeds, and his deeds bear the fruitage of character and destiny."

The above principle governs who we are, what we do and the results we get from life. So if we change who are, we change what we do and ultimately the result we get.

Permit me to mention here that principles which drive our behaviour give meaning to our lives and these principles enable us to engage in projects with our hearts and minds.

Our beliefs and values define who we are and what we do. Core values are relevant to the majority of areas in our life and they do affect what we say, think, and actions we take. Values are what make us the way we are, they drive us and provide motivation for how we live our lives. Values are the key to living a motivated, successful and rewarding life.

This is when awareness and responsibility comes into place.

CHAPTER 12

Path to Personal Creativity and Leadership

"Changes start off as thoughts, they are structured and communicated in pictures and words and become action."

- *Frances Coombes, Author of Teach Yourself – Self Motivation; p.51*

It's important for me to mention in this section the relevance of our thought process on creativity. In his book *Skills for the Future*, Robert B. Dilts, mentioned that the richness of our imagination comes from our ability to make maps in our minds. We build mental maps out of information from the five senses or representational systems: sight, sound, feeling, taste, and smell. Our senses constitute the form or structure of thinking as opposed to its content.

What's this implication of these assertions?

It means that every thought that you have, regardless of its content, is a function of pictures, sounds, feelings, smells or taste, and how those representations relate to one another. The result is that we are constantly linking together sensory representations to build and update our maps of reality. We make these maps based on feedback from our sensory experience.

According to Robert Dilts, "All act of creation involve the mobilization of your nervous system in order to interact with or change your environment." In the belief of Neuro-Linguistic Programming* (NLP), creativity is creativity regardless of where it's applied. What this means is that no matter the field of endeavour one is creative it can be relevant and transferable in another field. For example, the creative process that someone uses to prepare a meal might be relevant to creative process relating to organising a team or developing a new product.

At the heart of any creative and innovative endeavour is the need to be flexible. This is based on the law of requisite variety (Asby, 1956). This law stipulates that we need to be constantly exploring variations in the operations and processes that we use to get results. For example, process that has been effective in the past might not continue to be effective if the environment or system around it changes.

*NLP is a model of creativity was developed in California in the early 1970's. It's based upon the research relating to some very basic aspects of human experience. NLP was founded by two people, John Grinder, a linguist, and Richard Bandler who had formal training in Mathematics, but also practiced Gestalt therapy. As the name connotes NLP taps into three subject areas:

- Neuro – our nervous system, focuses on how the nervous system perceives, processes and performs (executes information)
- Linguistics- NLP is of the view that language is in some ways a product of the nervous system
- Programming – based on the idea that the processes of human learning, of memory, of creativity, are functions of programs – neurolinguistic programs that function more or less effectively to accomplish particular objectives and outcomes.

In a nutshell, according to Robert Dilt; "flexibility is needed to adapt and survive."

Levels of Creativity and Innovation

"That is what learning is. You suddenly understand something you've understood all your life but in a new way."

- *Doris Lessing*

Anthropologist Gregory Bateson identified five levels of learning and change – each level more abstract than the level below it but each having a greater degree of impact on the individual.

These levels roughly correspond to:

1. Who I **A**m – Identity   Who?

2. My **B**elief system – Values and Meanings   Why?

3. My **C**apabilities – Strategies and States   How?

4. What I **D**o or have **D**one – Specific Behaviours   What?

5. My Environment – External Constraints   Where?

                                                When?

Source: Dilts R. D. and Gino Bonissone Skills for the Future: Managing Creativity and Innovation (1993) - Defining the Scope of Creativity. p. 55

It's important to make the following clarification concerning the above model of learning and change as per the various levels.

The environment level – this the specific external conditions in which our behaviour takes place. There is the need for behaviours to be guided by inner map, plan or strategy, without which behaviour at this level would be likened to a knee jerk reaction, habits or rituals.

The capability level – here we are able to select, alter and adapt a class of behaviours to a wider range of situation. This requires some sort of intelligence positioning.

The beliefs and values level – at this level we may encourage, inhibit or generalize a particular strategy, plan or way of thinking.

The identity level – this consolidates whole system of beliefs and values in a sense of self.

On the whole even though each level becomes more removed from the specifics of behaviour and sensory experience, it actually has considerable widespread effect on our behaviour and experiences.

CHAPTER 13

Grow your self – constantly and consistently into a successful person

"Without continual growth and progress, such words as improvement, achievement, and success have no meaning."

Benjamin Franklin

Life is in a continual flux or change. You are a spiritual being first and foremost, you have a soul and you live in a body. There are four main dimensions to your being and these in turn impinges on your needs. These needs are spiritual need, physical need, mental need, and social need.

In order to meet these needs on a personal basis and still contribute your greatest skill and talent you need grow as a person. You need to constantly and consistently raise your standards, remove limiting believe and change your strategy in your journey to create your reality.

Imagine you grow yourself such that you in terms of who you are (your identity), what you are able to do (capability), and the result (outcome or experience you realize). Simply it means that you change your mind set, change what you are capable of doing and become more productive. This automatically raises your awareness to what is possible hence your perception. You become more responsible in your commitment and integrity of purpose.

If you gain more skill, more ability, more intelligence, a capacity to do things few people can do, think creatively and contribute in a massive scale you can earn more than you ever thought possible.

Becoming rich isn't about getting rich financially as about as about whom you need to become in character and mind, to get rich. The fastest way to get rich and stay rich is to work on developing YOU! The idea is to grow yourself into a successful person.

"No one can tell whether he is rich or poor by turning to his ledger. It is the heart that makes a man rich. He is **rich according** *to what he is, not according to what he has."*

Henry Ward Beecher

Your outer world is merely a reflection of your inner world. You could be metaphorically likened as the root and your results are the fruits. Growing yourself to a successful person entails acquiring the attributes you require inside out to live the life of your dream. Therefore, if grow yourself to become a successful person, in strength of character and mind, you will naturally be successful in anything and everything you do. You will grow the inner power and ability to choose any business or investment area and prosper therein.

In a nutshell growing yourself entails growing more and more in your thinking; never being satisfied in your present situation or circumstance. Becoming a successful person means that you will be able to do what you need to do, have what you want including lots of money.

According to T. Harv Eker; the author of, "Secrets of the Millionaire mind" "the goal of creating wealth is not primarily to have lots of money, the goal of creating wealth is to help you grow yourself into the person you can possibly be.". This in itself is mastery.

In conclusion, success is not a "what", it's "who." Who you are is totally trainable and learnable.

"We are what we repeatedly do. Excellence is not an act but habit."

- *Aristole*

Perhaps these quotes from Jack Welch, former Chairman and CEO of General Electric puts this captures the idea in this section:

"Before you are a leader, success is about growing yourself. When you become success is all about growing others."

CHAPTER 14

The Triads to great wealth
3T's to great fortune – fabulous riches and wealth AND how to unlock them

"Imagination is the beginning of creation. You imagine what you desire, you will what you imagine, and at last create what you will."
-   George Bernard Shaw

Before we can be able to become proficient and productive in the act of creativity and innovation, we need to first and foremost have very good understanding about the working of the human mind. This understanding is not enough, but we need to know how to exploit this part of our being in bringing to birth our desire through three of the daily habits we use daily to make sense of our inner and outer worlds; namely, thinking, feeling and action.

We also need to make the most effective use of our God given talents and be aware of how to use our talent to achieve the outcomes we desire.

The productive use of our time is very important, and this requires us to master how best to apportion our time towards the realisation of productive outcomes. The idea of the way we use our time is very subjective but on the whole it is important to know how to use our time to contribute meaningfully to life's goals – both for ourselves and for others.

In this section we are going to look at the three important resources that are freely given to us which we can use to tap in to the myriads of opportunities all around us. Mastering the use of these tools could be the difference between unlocking the abundance of rich resources to wealth that are all around us.

Thought – your most valuable asset

"You become what you think about most of the time."
Earl Nightingale

Thoughts are moving forces; great forces for that matter. Thoughts are about things – people, ideas (data/information), dreams, etc. Thoughts of wealth attract wealth. Therefore, if you desire wealth, you must think of those thoughts that will put you along this course. Thoughts of health attract health. Also thought of being wise enables us to align with the Spirit of God that gives wisdom.

We can change who, what and where we are in our lives simply by changing how and what we think about on consistent basis.

You are where and who you are right now as the sum total of all your thought to this point in your life. But it's up to this point.

Your level of success and achievement in any area of life is in direct proportion to your ability and willingness to direct your thoughts into effective planning and organised action towards a specific goal combined with a strong reason WHY you're doing it in the first place.

"Where success is concerned, people are not measured in inches or pounds, or college degree, or family background; they are measured by size of their thinking."

- *David Schwartz*

The successful person does not react – but think. You need to operate from your conscious mind and think. When faced with any situation, your subconscious (habitual mind) will try to deal with it and you react. The mind is often compared to an iceberg, with the conscious mind being 10% above the waterline and the subconscious the 90% that is submerged.

"Thinking is the operation skill through which intelligence acts upon experience."

Edward De **Bono**

If you want to further discover the path to a changed life read this article here:

http://bit.ly/14yYidX

You can also explore other articles on thinking: The Strangest Secret by Earl Nightingale here:

http://bit.ly/13ZdxNM

Talent – your most valuable gift

"...The most successful people build their career around their natural talents and passion. And they build a cabinet of people with different natural talent from their own."

- *Blaire Palmer*

Achievement is usually talent plus preparation.

Each person that comes into this world has been endowed by with God given ability called talent which will you to profit from life as well as contribute meaningfully to impact others. In every field of knowledge or human endeavour there are people that have discovered their God given talents and have worked very hard to sharpen this ability – to use their talent to create opportunities that will improve other people's lives. They have been rewarded for their contribution because of the products /services that they have created to add value to other people's lives.

What is it that makes the difference between the creative person and the less creative person?

Well, it's not any special power but greater knowledge of practised expertise and motivation to acquire it.

"Practice isn't the thing you do once you're good. It's the thing you do that makes you good."

- *Malcolm Gladwell – Author of Outliers – the story of success.*

In a study of male professionals from diverse field such as singing, acting, writing, computer programming, music, aviation, and fire fighting. It was revealed by the Cambridge Handbook of Expertise Performance that of all the more superb performers that expertise is made not burn. It is the amount and quality of practice which influences the level of expertise people achieve rather than any innate gift.

Margaret A Boden in her book "The Creative Mind" reported that: "Talent which matter include the ability to engage other people, to communicate clearly, to assimilate information, to lean to generate and make decisions."

It is worthy of note here, to mention that the key to creating passion in one's life is to find your unique talents and your special role and purpose in the world.

According to David McNally, in his book "Even Eagles Need A Push, "people perform at their best when contributing their talents to something they believe in."

What is your talent? Have you considered how best to develop it? This key to performing excellently in your chosen career or vocation is to work hard to develop your talent and use it to serve others. Perhaps, this is described succinctly by this quote from Stephen King.

"Talent is cheaper than table salt. What separates the talented individual from the successful one is a lot of hard work."

Time – your most valuable resource

Time itself is the heart of true wealth and ultimate freedom.

"Quite literally, time IS money – time IS life – therefore time must be considered the most precious thing that we own."
-Benjamin Franklin

Throughout history there are men who have been very productive on the way that they apportioned time to productive activities that added value or contributed to other people's lives. One such individual is Benjamin Franklin who was called "the father of time management.

He summed his philosophy about time through these statements:

- Time is the one thing that when lost can never be recovered.
- Time is necessary to achieve all else in this world.
- Time is the most squandered and most wasted resource and whose full value of time is something most people never fully understand or appreciate.

Each person is freely given the same amount of time every day. Let's look at time more closely. We have sixty minutes in every hour, twenty four hours in a day, and one hundred and sixty eight days in a week.

Time is of great essence. If not for anything, it's a measurable unit and resource for us to create value.

The Scripture captures succinctly in the Book of Ecclesiastes chapter 3:1; "To *everything* there is a *season*, and *a time* to *every purpose* under heaven"

If you think intently on this passage you will observe that time is to be apportioned. But how do you apportion time? Underneath the apportionment of time is the purpose; the reason for the time is the season. If you go further to investigate this passage of the Scripture; Ecclesiastes 8:5b said, "And a wise man's heart discerneth both time and judgement." If look at verse 6, it reads; "Because to every purpose there is *time and judgement*, therefore the misery of man is great upon it.

You will see there is great need for us to have wisdom on how to use our time. We need to walk wisely on our use of time. It means the way we act towards time. Do we use it frugally towards a productive end or prodigally towards a wasteful endeavour?

Time is your most valuable resource. It is a bank account that we all have in common, but is an account which is peculiar in nature. You cannot deposit in it. You can only withdraw. There is no statement telling you how much you have left in it. It is of course the bank account of time. So we need to seize the day.

There is never any time but NOW, but there will never be ant time but NOW. For you to have what you want to achieve you must begin NOW.

It's worthy of note that no matter how wonderful the future may look to you at this time, you must now place your feet firmly on the ground of the present moment.

Victor Hugo has this to say about time and planning: "He who every morning plans the transaction of the day, and follows out the plans carries a thread that will guide him through labyrinth of the most busy life. The underlying arrangement of his time is like a ray of light which darts itself through all of his occupation. But when no plan is laid, the deposition of time is surrendered merely to chance or incidents, chaos will soon reign."

> Labyrinth: a structure containing winding passages through which it is hard to find one's way, a maze.

We need to use our time wisely, to pursue the important things that help us to meet our goals in life.

Develop the habit of doing the daily easy to do list

The following three habits of time management program were given to Charles Schwab by Ivy Lee

1. At the end of a day draw up a list of all the jobs you need to do the following day.
2. Now number them in order of importance.
3. The following day when you start work, start at number one. Keep at it until it is complete. Then move to number 2 and keep at it until it is complete, and so on.

Perhaps this anonymous poem sums up the way and manner we need to relate with time in our daily lives.

Take time to work –

It is the price of success.

Take time to think –

It is the source of power.

Take time to play –

It is the secret of perpetual youth.

Take time to read –

It is the fountain of wisdom.

Take time to be friendly –

It is the road to happiness.

Take time to love and be loved –

It is nourishment for the soul.

Take time to share –

It is too short a life to be selfish.

Take time to laugh –

It is the music of the heart.

Take time to dream –

It is hitching your wagon to the stars.

CHAPTER 15

3 steps to creating your own good fortune

"You and I have the same power at our disposal every moment of the day – (the power of decision). At any moment, the questions we ask ourselves can shape our perception of who we are, what we are capable of and what we're willing to do to achieve our dreams."

- *Anthony Robins*

The above quote captures the thoughts of Anthony Robbins as he sets himself up to new standards that ultimately changed his life and business landscape.

He asked himself these very important questions:

"How can I add even more value and help people even while I slept?"

"How can I reach people in a way that is not limited to my physical presence?"

These questions opens new opportunities which may never have been possible without challenging himself to contribute more through adding more value to people's lives in a new and innovative way.

With these questions came the idea of his franchise operations in which more people could represent him across the United States. Later on, a year later these questions resulted in him coming up with the IDEA of producing television infomercials.

From the above story, we can see very clearly how Anthony Robbins, became, rich, famous and wealthy through contribution of his diverse skills and talents to empower other people's lives.

Ask yourself this simple question:

How can you increase, the value of what I do ten or fifteen times?

What systems can you adopt to distribute this value you've created?

The above question calls for you to see yourself in a new way – raise your standard of what's possible and to intelligently position yourself as well as commit to making your new reality a possibility.

Lessons learned from the wealthy and successful people over the ages shows that you don't need to be creative, innovative – entrepreneurial so as to be rich and wealthy.

Wealth is also created by distribution. The secret of the most of the world's richest people was that they created distribution systems to sale the values they or others have created to many people.

- **Identify a core human desire / need**

Is there a way you can use your knowledge, life's experience or hobby to solve a core human need or want based on Maslow's hierarchy of need?

- **Find a new technology for solving the core desire / need and /or want**

What new technology can you use to solve the core desire or need of your prospects?

During his time Earle Prevette used telephone to sow the idea of life insurance in the minds of people. What technology can you adopt today to solving or meeting the solutions of your clients?

Look at the options we have with the internet? Is there a way you can use the internet to leverage the way you solve the problems of your clients?

- ### Find a new way to market this core desire / need

What ways can you package and sale this information to a large audience in a very short time?

Have you considered an information product – teaching something via products, which can be delivered as prints, audio, or video?

You need to take massive action to make these dreams a reality.

New knowledge has no worth to your business unless it's implemented and acted upon.

How can you share your greatest gift or talent in a tangible form by way of products, programs or services for others to implement?

I leave you with this quote from Henry Ford:

"The whole secret of a successful life is to find out what it is in one's destiny to do and then do it."

You need to realize that it's desire not ability that determines your success. You can get anything, you can do anything if you really want to, and the only limitation is what you put on yourself.

Successful people are happy and fulfilled individuals. They love what they do, because what they do is an expression of their gift and talent.

What can you do with your skills, talent, passion and experience?

"Leadership is the capacity to translate vision into reality."

- *Warren Bennis*

You can read my article on how to increase your productivity here:

http://bit.ly/15qVlf9

CHAPTER 16

Wealth and wealth creation – a quick preview

What is wealth?

"Wealth is the product of man's ability to think."

- *Ayn Rand*

Wallace D Wattles, the author of "" has this to say about wealth:

Wealth culture consists of making constructive use of people and things in your environment.

From the above prescription on wealth it is important for us to focus attention on the idea; "constructive use of people in your environment." This suggests a way of thinking or being and intelligent use of resources in one's environment.

Intelligence after all is the capacity and ability to size up yourself and to organise them into a workable plan that you may share in life's abundance.

Let us look closely to some of the words mentioned above – capacity and ability. The meaning of these words could give us more insight to their relevance.

Capacity has one of the four meanings:

- The maximum capacity that can be contained or produced
- Maximum amount
- The ability or talent; power or potential

- A positive role assigned or assumed

- The quality of electricity that a battery, motor etc. can deliver under particular conditions.

Ability has been described as follows:

- Ability (the physical, mental or legal power to do something)

- Natural or acquired competence in doing something

- Skill – a natural talent or aptitude

Source: The Penguin English Dictionary

Wealth creation secret – a preamble

"Wealth is when small effort produces big result. Poverty is when big effort produces small results."

- *Anonymous*

From the above introductions on wealth, it is clear that the wealth creation is ability. Essentially, it's the ability to take something that has little value and convert it into something of significantly greater value. Those who are wealthy today have learned to transform something common into something precious and have reaped the economics of financial reward that comes from this transformation.

Wealth creation is share entrepreneurial skill of creative problem solving. At the heart of this is to find a way to sell the solution of the problem you solved to many people.

The key to wealth is to be more valuable.

Devise a way to consistently add value to people's lives and you will proper. Entrepreneurs create two forms of values:

- Add value to customers by increasing the quality of their lives through use of products
- Their products create jobs

Wealth is the result of effective evaluations

The above quote was made by Anthony Robbins in his book, "Awaken the giant within."

The following questioned are of importance here.

What does it mean to make evaluation?

What then is effective evaluation?

Before I answer these questions I want to take you back to what one of the world's great investors – John Templeton; had to say when he was asked the reason for his success.

He said; "My ability to evaluate the true value of an investment."

He's simply saying that his success was based on his ability to make an effective evaluation of an investment.

So in back to our question on the meaning of the word evaluation: Evaluation is the structured interpretation and giving of meaning to predict or actual impacts of proposals or results. It looks at original objectives, and at what is either predicted or what was accomplished and how it was accomplished. So evaluation can be **formative** that is taking place during the development of a concept or proposal, project or organization, with the intention of improving the value or effectiveness of the proposal, project, or organisation. It can also be **summative**, drawing lessons from a completed action or project or an organisation at a later point in time or circumstance.

Source: http://en.wikipedia.org/wiki/Evaluation#cite_note-2

Evaluation is the highest level of thinking skill and the aim is to add value to an objective. It is subject specific.

Factors that affect our evaluation

There are certain factors that affect our evaluation.*

---

1. Mental and emotional state

2. The questions you ask

3. Hierarchy of values

4. Beliefs

5. References

---

*Taken from the book - *"Awaken the giant within",* by Anthony Robbins

Mental and emotional state

The mental and emotional state that you are in at the moment you made an evaluation could impact the outcome of your evaluation and hence the result you get. One major key to superior evaluation, then is to make certain that when we're making decisions about what things mean and what to do, we're in an extremely resourceful state of mind and emotion rather than survival mode.

The questions we ask

The questions you ask reflects your thought process at the point in time and does impact the answers you get and possibly the results you get. According to Anthony Robbins, "questions are the laser of human consciousness, they concentrate our focus and determine what we feel and do."

Hierarchy of value

Your values are those things – intangible and intangible, people, information etc. that are important to you. Things that you thing about, do yearn to have or become could reveal the things that are valuable to you and therefore could be basis to your passion. It'll be good if you know the things that are of great value of you since they impact on the long run the results you get from life.

Beliefs

Your belief is an idea that has taken "hold of you." Belief determines how you do life. Most of your belief could have come from your childhood may be form associations you had. They may eventually impact on the way you do life – that is, your norm and values. If your belief concerning certain aspects of your life is not working for you then you change them – throw them away and cultivate the new belief systems that will help you to create the future you so greatly desire. If you want to change your belief you have to change your thinking.

Reference

Your reference is the repertoire of resources for repository of information or knowledge that help you to make informed decisions concerning situations in life. If you have watched the TV program who wants to be a millionaire; in most of the question the contestant is given an opportunity to phone a friend in order to find answered to a question. This is a case of reference.

You can increase your access to such knowledge by becoming more knowledgeable or through the development of expertise in a particular field of knowledge. You can learn from experts in a particular field of knowledge, you can leverage your knowledge through development of master minds – people in your interest groups that you can share information with to impact your business outcome.

On the whole you should not allow your past and present conditioning to rob you of the vision of a great future where can create the opportunity to prosper from your passion.

A story about wealth creation to take to heart

Anthony Robbins is a top life coach. In his book, *"Awaken the giant within",* he describes three principles that he adopted to become wealthy.

1. Special knowledge – he mastered skills and abilities that could instantaneously increase the quality of life of virtually anyone;

2. The he figured out a way to share this information and these skills with a large number of people in a short period of time;

3. As a result he prospered not only economically but financially as well.

If you really desire to earn more money where you are today, one of the simplest ways is to ask yourself the following questions:

1. How can I be worth more to yourself or organisation?
2. How can I achieve this fit in less time?
3. How can I add tremendous amount of value – long term value to my organisation?
4. Are there some ways that I could cut cost and create quality?
5. What new system could I develop?
6. What new technology could I use that would allow the company to produce or distribute its services more effectively?

It is also important to mention here the tenets surrounding the law of income.

The Law of Income

"An amazing axiom about life. The more value you create the more income we seem to generate."

- *Nido Qubein*

You will be paid in direct proportion to the value you deliver according to the market place. There are four factors that determine your value in the market place. These factors are namely supply, demand, quality and quantity. The key to unlock your profitability in any market place is to increase quantity of the value you add. For most people this is the greatest challenge.

The quantity factor simply addresses how much of your value you do actually deliver in the market place. What this means in real terms is to ask; how many people do you actually serve or effect?

In conclusion, if you can help people to do more with less, then you are truly empowering them and you will be empowered economically as well, as long as you put yourself in a position to do so.

Three important lessons about the laws of wealth

"But remember the Lord your God, for it is He who gives you the ability to produce wealth."

Deuteronomy 8:18

1. Realise that everything you can think of exists now; otherwise you could not think about it. There is no lack of anything and there shall be no envy or jealousy between men. There is enough of everything for everyone that lives.

2. Realise that all things belong to God's creation and that you can only have a temporary use of them. There is no limit on your desires and you can have use of anything the ability can create.

3. Realise that all things are distributed to those who have desires, but must be applied to formulate plans to claim the desire.

It's clear from the forgoing as John Earl Shoaff summed it up: "Life never withholds anything from anyone. Love, health, wealth and companionship; all these exists in infinite abundance."

You can read articles on Wealth and wealth creation ability by following this link:

http://bit.ly/1oyQHW4

http://bit.ly/YnjV9d

In conclusion listen to what Henry Ford had to say concerning wealth:

Wealth is created from service, wealth only comes from service. Ford said, "Wealth, like happiness, is never attained when sought after directly. It comes as a by-product of providing a useful service." Who are you serving?

Source: *http://bit.ly/15kyX5y*

CHAPTER 17

Two forms of imagination faculties – creative and constructive or synthetic imagination

Creative imagination

"An idea is salvation by imagination"

-   *Frank Lloyd Wright*

The creative imagination takes the elements of the past as reproduced by memory and rearranges them. It forms new combinations out of the materials of the past. It forms new ideas, emotions and their accompanying impulses to muscular activity, the elements of mental "complexes". It combines the elements into new and original mental pictures, the creations of the inventive mind. The ability of access and employ this type of creative mind is available to all professionals and not limited to the poet, the artist, the inventor, or the philosopher. It is the application of this imagination in specialised areas of knowledge that leads to particular inventions, breakthroughs or valued solutions to problems in such fields. Understanding application of creative imagination in any field of human endeavour is the key to great riches and wealth. In his book Applied Psychology in business Warren Hilton bluntly had this to say about creative imagination.

"The fact is that no man can succeed in any pursuit until he has creative imagination."

The development and application of creative imagination has been the fundamental attribute to most progress that man has accomplished within the past century; without such stride in this development in creative imagination, he would still be living in caves. And the great inventions of present civilisation; ships, computers, internet, electric cars, businesses, would not have been possible without creative imagination. It is important to mention that nothing exists in the entire world that had not a previous counterpart in the mind of him who designed it. And also it is important to remember that at the back of all creative minds is God.

He has given us the ability to create wealth

It is through this faculty that "hunches" and instincts are received. It is through this faculty that all new ideas are handed over to man. You can also receive thought vibrations from the minds of others are received

The constructive or synthetic imagination

Constructive or synthetic imagination enables you to devise, project, forecast and devise means to attain your desired position of attainment. This type of imagination is very important in business since in any form of work it enables you to imagine the best that might be, and stretches your mind to conceive it, and then devise someway to attain it. Understanding of the technique to sharpen this faculty of the mind – constructive imagination is important because it is the gate way to formulate the means to transmute the desire to its object form. Transformation of intangible impulse, desire into tangible reality for example, money, calls for the use of a plan, or plans. These plans can be formed with the aid of imagination, and mainly, with the constructive imagination.

Applications of the imagination faculties to riches and wealth creation

"There are no limitations to the mind except those we acknowledge. Both poverty and riches are the offspring of the mind."
- *Napoleon Hill*

People will normally say to you that knowledge is power.

If your knowledge cannot be applied to add value to one who needs it or provide advice to someone; of what use is it? You are paid for what you do with what you know as well as advice you give to people with it; in fact the value you create with your knowledge. Knowledge only becomes power when it is organised into definite plan of action, and directed to a definite end. The desire to transmute desire into monetary equivalent is made possible through specialised knowledge of the service, merchandise or profession which you intend to offer in return for fortune.

According to Napoleon Hill, the accumulation of fortunes calls for POWER, and power acquired through highly organised and intelligently directed knowledge but this knowledge does not have to be in the possession of man who accumulates the fortune.

The only ingredient required for this capability is imagination.

Imagination is the quality needed to combine specialised knowledge with ideas in the form of organised plans designed to yield riches.

According to Hilton Warren in his book "Power of Mental Imagery"; "mind And mind alone; possess the inscrutable power to create."

Mind is supreme. Mind shapes and controls matter. Every concrete thing in the world is the product of the thinking consciousness. The diverse richly presented works of art are the physical expression of the artist's dream. The great factory with its whirling mechanisms and glowing furnaces, according to warren Hilton, is the material manifestations of the promoter's financial imaginations. The beautiful, tall and extravagant displays of sky scrapers parading the air of industrialised cities of worlds are testament of the creative imaginations of the architects and builders. All these examples and more are thought moulded out of formless matter. Mind, finite and infinite is eternally creative and creating in the organisation of formless mater and material forces, into concrete realities. Creative Imagination is an absolute prerequisite for material achievement. The business man must scheme and plan, and devise and foresee. He must create in imagination today the result he is to achieve tomorrow. He must combine all the elements of his past experiential complexes into mental picture of future events as he would have them.

Warren Hilton reasoned that riches are the material realisation of a financial imagination; whereas, the wealth of the world is but the sum total of the contribution of creative thoughts of the successful men of all ages.

CHAPTER 18

7 steps to any worthwhile and great accomplishment

Unleash the power of goal setting

"Setting goals is the first step in turning the invisible into visible – the foundation of all successes in life."

- Anthony Robbins

Desire is the fuel that drives you forward towards the destination which is represented by your goals.

The best advice you will get about getting what you want from live begins with the need to set goals. It is important to mention that establishing personal goals in all areas of areas of your life is extremely important. Before anything else it will put you in good stead to know that at the heart of learning to soar is the understanding of the principle of contribution.

From this principle of contribution stems the facts that rewards follow service – getting follows giving – and making an impression follows making a difference.

Therefore, before determining what it is you want, you need to clarify what it is you offer.

In order to bring to birth the contributions that you desire to bring into the world, there is the need to look into the skills you need to "express your voice", according to Stephen R Covey, in his book "The 8th Habit."

Great achievers who have made significant contributions, and have made things happen in their field of endeavours have something in common. Basically, through their persistent effort and inner struggles, they have greatly expanded their four native human intelligence or capacities.

From my point of view this is real choice and freedom; according to Walter Lippman:

"A useful definition of liberty is obtained only by seeking the principle of liberty in the main business of human life, that is to say, in the process which men educate their responses and learn to control their environment."

The highest manifestations of these four intelligences are: for the mental, vision; for the physical, discipline; for the emotional, passion; for the spiritual conscience. These manifestations also represent our highest means of expressing our voice. They cannot be looked at in isolation but could be seen to be bound as one single whole. Understanding this is the key to fulfilling you destiny and attaining your integrity. We are going to look at each of these attributes very closely because understanding them holds the key towards our ability to realise our personal goals and aspirations. Your ability to any great accomplishments depends on your ability to master the synergistic application of these four attributes. You need to know how to allow all of them work in harmony for you.

Vision – see the big picture

Earle Prevette wrote the following about vision:

"Vision is the camera of the imagination and supplies the film to register the image. Vision is one of the most important faculties – it develops foresight and turns hindsight into profit."

In his book "The heart of success: making it in business without losing your life, he reasoned that vision has to grow, and that if you want to see a vision grow you have to fulfil three conditions:

- You need to have a seed
- You need to actually plant it
- You must remember to water it

Vision without action = hallucination

You need to have a seed

You have to realise that vision has to do with the "what" that you need to accomplish. It is the seed of an idea, dream, thought, and desire of what you want to accomplish. This has to be very clear to you that you will literally be able to describe it thoroughly.

You need to actually plant it

Just like a seed is planted into the soil in order for it to germinate; you need to plant the seed of your idea in your mind such as to set its growth and development into motion.

You must remember to water it

For the seed to germinate and grow it needs to be nurtured and given it fair share of the natural sunlight, water, warmth and humidity for it to grow. Watering the seed makes it possible for the seed to receive available moisture required to trigger and sustain the photosynthetic and respiratory process important for the plant growth. Again in the light of your ideas you need to look out for those variable which are as a matter of necessity required for the idea to thrive.

Discipline – give it your best shot

According to Stephen R Covey, discipline comes from being "discipled" to a person or cause.

Towards any great accomplishment you need vision as well the ability to be disciplined. Have you seen any successful professional in any field of human endeavour? They are disciplined. They have a way of thinking and behaving which enables them to deliver excellence time after time. Discipline is the gap between your dream and its accomplishment. You need to ask yourselves what it will take as well as your commitment and determination to follow through. Underneath this is for you to believe that you are 100% responsible for the result you get. You need to realise that you can have the beliefs and have the goals, but if you don't have the daily habits, the daily discipline or the weekly or monthly disciplines depending on your goals you will never achieve your goals.

Passion – the fuel to your desire

"Passion is the blood that feels the veins of your creative self; it provides the circulatory system that allows your imagination to breathe."

-Jeff VanderMeer, Author, *"Booklife – Digital strategies and survival tips for the 21st century writers."*

Passion is the fuel that energises you towards accomplishing your dream, in bad time and good time. Passion provides you with the spiritual fervour to move in bad and good time.

Conscience – size up your self

The conscience is the "heart of the matter." It is often referred to as the God's spirit searching through your deepest motive.

Personal Goal Setting – How to turn your idea to reality
"The best way to predict the future is to create it."
- Peter Drucker
We've mentioned about the about discovering your passion and in this section we'll be looking at a simple exercise on goal setting and how to turn your passion to reality. It could also mean the strategies, tactics you need to move from where you are to where you want to be.

A strategy is what you're going to do; a tactics is how you're going to do. The strategies and tactics may simply boil down to doing some research and asking the right questions. For example, there must have been people who have done what you're trying to do or a book that has been written to guide you through on the ways to follow. Hence, in most case it is a matter of reinventing the wheel.

Therefore there're 3 things that you need to change and achieve goals:

1. Knowledge of what you intend to do
2. Instruction – the strategies and tactics of what to do
3. Environment – the accountability or responsibility to take ownership of the goal and stay on track toward its achievement.

Seven step goal setting exercise

The section describes the seven–step goal setting exercise that you can us to set and achieve goals on anything imaginable that you've set your heart to achieve. The seven steps summarize the best techniques that have been devised for setting goals, streamlining your activities and enabling you to accomplish and execute excellently.

Step No.1 – decide exactly what you want and write it down.

Here you need to be as descriptive enough as possible and succinctly describe the goal you wish to attain. This activity alone moves you into the top 3 per cent of adults and can change your life for ever. This is a very important step and clarity is the key here. You need to be very clear in being able to describe you intention, objective, purpose or what it is you desire to accomplish.

In 1953 study of Yale University graduating class where 20 years later, the 3% who wrote actually wrote down their goals were found to be worth more than the other 95% put together.

"ONLY BY WRITING DOWN YOUR GOAL ON PAPER CAN YOU HARNESS YOUR SUBCONSCIOUS MIND TO GO TO WORK TO REALIZE YOUR GOAL."

- **Frank Tibolt, Author, A *Touch of Greatness***

Step No.2 – set a deadline for your goal.

Set sub deadlines if necessary. Be very careful about the timelines and what you intend to accomplish every day, week, month and year. The more specific you are about your deadline and your dated, the more you will accomplish - and sooner than you expect.

Step No.3 – determine the obstacles that you will have to overcome to achieve your goal.

As you move in the direction of achieving your goal, there are considerations, feelings, and roadblocks that impinge on your progress towards the achievement of your goal. In his book, "how to get from where you are to where you want to be", Jack Canfield, described the consideration as those thoughts from within that holds you back, the feelings are the fear, and the roadblocks are the barriers in your present environment that prevent your dream taking off. What are the choke points or bottlenecks that determine the speed at which you achieve your goal? Why aren't you at your goal already? Of all the barriers that you have to overcome, what is the largest single one? Start with that.

Step No.4 – determine the additional knowledge, skills and abilities you will need to reach goal.

There is always the need for you to figure out who you need to become so as to achieve your goal. Hence it may require a new knowledge acquisition, development or improvement on your skills and abilities. Either way the onus is on you to identify the opportunities you are faced with, your motivation to attain to your goal and finding out the means at your disposal to making it happen.

Step No. 5 – determine the people, groups and organisations whose help you will require to achieve your goal.

Being able to identify people who will enable you to realise your goal is key to its accomplishment. This is important because you may not have the skill set necessary to the realisation of your dream but the ability to work with other people who are more proficient in the skills you are deficient in could be useful. Most of the time it requires your ability to share your vision to the team of people you will be working with and making it clear the roles they are to play in the scheme of things.

Step No. 6 – make a plan to achieve your goal.

Make a list of the obstacles you will have to overcome, the additional knowledge and skills you will have acquire and the people whose help you will need. Organise the list into a plan based on priority and sequence.

Step No.7 – and perhaps the most important of all – take action immediately on your plan.

The implementation of your plan through taking massive action on daily, weekly, monthly, and yearly basis followed by a mechanism to monitor and access your progress is important to the achievement of your goal. Most of the time, you may have the need to chunk your tasks and activities into manageable segments so to be on top of your project.

Here are recommendations for accelerating your progress toward your goals:

1-Don't waste your time on unimportant, trivial things.

2-Focus on tasks that are important and contribute to your success.

3-Treasure your time like, as Dan Kennedy says, the gold in Fort Knox.

4-Get busy. Most successful people I know are busy.

5-Work hard. Whoever said "work smart, not hard," was wrong. Successful people work smart and hard.

6-Focus on what you do best. Farm out everything else.

7-Don't feel you have to do something just because someone asks you. Learn to say no.

8-Set priorities, because your bandwidth, like everyone else's, is limited.

9-Become obsessed with ROTI - return on time invested - for every activity you undertake.

10-There is plenty of success advice out there from people who are not successful. Ignore it.

Source: Article from Accelerate your success with focus by Bob Bly – Copywriter and Consultant.

CHAPTER 19

Power of Leverage – Achieve more with less effort

"The only way to REALLY raise your standard of living is to leverage your talents, your gifts, your interests and your hobbies to create a product or service that you can sell to increasing numbers of people and free yourself from the cycle of trading time for money."

Walt F.J. Goodridge – Author, Passion for Profit

As a single person there is a limit to the extent of what you are going to achieve as an individual. You need to be intelligent in your ability to notice and use the resources all around you to your advantage. Have you imagined the process the get achievers in different fields of life use to leverage their effort? You need to learn to under the principle of leverage so as to impact on you productivity and profitability – your bottom line. Some of these ideas have been gleaned from successful entrepreneurs who have used these same techniques.

1. Surround yourself with like minds

Someday this will be true for all of us:
Our network will equal our net worth.
TIM SANDERS

Mentors

A single conversation across the table with a wise man is worth a month's study of books.

CHINESE PROVERB

Essentially a mentor is one who has been through what you desire to accomplish. He or she has established expertise on a particular area of knowledge. You have the opportunity of learning from the individual and this will drastically reduce your learning period. Ultimately, this is an opportunity to leverage and empower you to achieve more in less time.

Coaches

Coaching is a method of facilitating another person's learning, development and performance. As you surround yourself with coaches they will help you to:

Find your own solution to your problem

Develop your skills

Change your limiting behaviour

Change your attitude, and

Change your performance.

Surrounding yourself with supportive people will help you to achieve faster and in less time.

Coaching is about removing limiting beliefs and keeping the client convinced of his / her ability to make positive change happen.

2. **Create a formidable team - Mastermind groups/accountability partners**

The realisation of your vision will depend on you being able to have an army of people who are good in those thing you are not very proficient in doing. The idea of mastermind groups was mentioned in Napoleon Hill book, Think and Grow Rich; it was attributed to Andrew Carnegie who claimed that his success was based on intercourse of ideas from brilliant minds better than himself. The meeting of the mind in shared interest results in a third mind quite superior than the original thought.

Most people's lives are a direct reflection of their peer groups.
ANTHONY ROBBINS

Your second form of leverage is to acquire a team. Together, you all achieve more, faster, easier. You can spot one another's blind spots. You can encourage discouraged team members. They can encourage you when you are down. They fill in the gaps in your skill sets. They can be strong where you're weak. As a team, you all run faster. A4-by-4 relay team runs the mile about two second faster than the individual runner. If you want speed you need a team.

3. **S**ave **Y**our **S**elf **T**ime **E**nergy **M**oney

Your sixth form of leverage is systems. Every millionaire has systematized , stream lined, and organized the processes of wealth. The most efficient form of information transfer is to learn your mentors system and follow it-whether you've chosen real estate, the stock market, business, or the internet. Learn the system.

When the combined force of mentors, teams, networks, infinite networks, tools, and systems is applied to a strong, long lever, miracles can happen in minutes.

You can rest assured that if you devote your time and attention to
the highest advantages of others, the Universe will support you,
always and only in the nick of time.
R. BUCKMINSTER FULLER

Your fourth form of leverage is the infinite network. There is a spiritual connection that links us all up. This is the realm of coincidence, serendipity, chance, a twist of fate. Tapping into the infinite network is the ultimate form of leverage.

Your fifth form of leverage is the use of tools and skills. Millionaires use the tools of wealth-computers, the internet, e-mail-for fast communications, fast calculations, and fast decisions. If you want a speedy result, you need instant information.

Invest in yourself

"Work harder on yourself than do on your job."
-Jim Rohn

You need to constantly and consistently invest in your personal and professional development. If you stop learning you stop growing and if you stop seize to contribute and add value to your life then you're in for a downward spiral. To invest in yourself you need to continually work in yourself to be learning, growing and contributing person. It requires you to expand your means of who you want to become, do and have. Indeed to grow you to a successful person.

According to Larry Wilson, you don't need to show success to need to be success.

You need to adopt the concept of constant self-improvement. You have to seek new ideas to consider, new methods to tests, and new skills to learn and master. This process makes you a more valuable human being and gives you the opportunity to serve others and yourself with great confidence, broader vision and great depth of experience.

You have to constantly be aware of and open to new opportunities. For example, you can become adept at being able to see patterns and opportunities for progress in new opportunities. You will be able to be a keen observer; with a critical mind like a crime investigator. Any time new opportunities present themselves you could pose this question:

"Is there some other way I can apply the newly observed information, the newly revealed fact to the task at hand and create something completely new and profitable?"

Always look out for an opportunity to see how you can change, grow and contribute as a person. Cultivate the norm of can do attitude and always purpose to deliver excellence in your outcome. These will impact on who you are, what you do and the result you get.

CHAPTER 20

Fortune Makers Program – Discover your own good fortune making mountain

"Converting knowledge into profit is an acquired skill."
- *Kriston Thompson, Founder, SpeakServeGrow.com*

Your business is the intersection between what you enjoy doing and what people will pay for.
Before beginning to describe the stages required for creating your own fortune mountain, I want to make it clear that you need to understand three things:

The ability to identify a product niche

The ability of create products that sale

The ability to create compelling copies to sell your products

You need to be knowledgeable about online marketing – branding and identity

Internet marketing – traffic, leads, and income generation.

The ability to market the products – on line, off line or both

The ability to monetize your product

For the purpose of this section my interest is on creating and marketing your idea, knowledge or passion as information products. Information products are information packaged in different formats that can be accessed based on our perceptions. For example, they could be in form of video, audios or texts.

I want to you to remember the key proposition to making your own fortune – when the idea creator meets an idea seller. Imagine how your productivity and profitability will if you can develop your gift and talent and transform it into a form as to solve people's problem. The idea here is for you to be able to package you knowledge, experience or ideas about those needs that are overarching to your prospects and package and market them in a form that they can implement. This is the domain of information marketing.

According to Robert Skrob, information marketing consultant, " information marketing is a small business for small entrepreneurs that's one – quarter *personality* and *entertainment* in the same way a great radio show engages his audience, one – quarter *cheerleader* encouraging your subscribers to take the next step towards their goals; one –quarter marketing expert in generating new customers and keeping the one you have, and one - quarter publishing great information for subscribers on the web, in newsletters, through creating and doing seminars."

On the whole you can learn, develop and perform excellently as an information marketer by learning how to gather, organise, package and distribute great content to your chosen audience. The key idea to profitability in your area of expertise is to learn how to monetise your product in your chosen market place.

Magic formulae for personal success -3 steps to turn your passion to profit

According to *Frank Tibolt, author of* *A Touch of Greatness*: "Whether you want to get rich, become a star salesman, a top executive or entertainer, your ONLY right starting step is to find or develop some

OVERMASTERING GOAL, VISION OR PURPOSE TO **DRAW AND DRIVE** YOU TO SUCCESS. Otherwise you'll fall by the wayside as all "average" folks do.

This is the bedrock of personal success. What does this entail?

The idea here is to find a need / desire that you deeply care about (passion) and devise ways to satisfy it. Here are three steps to follow:

➢ Have a purpose

➢ Find out how by achieving your purpose, you can serve others.

➢ Devise a way to spread the knowledge using a platform and monetize it.

Leo Angart's Vision Workshop – a story to illustrate the principle above

Leo Angart had a purpose. He wanted to let the world know that poor eyesight and wearing glasses is not an particularly due to the ageing process. He was passionate to share his experience from benefiting from the knowledge that he used to correct his sight. He applied the information he saw from reading a book written by William Bates using energy exercises. By applying his special knowledge in hypnosis and healing he developed a recipe for improving eyesight the natural way. He claimed that he has 20/20 vision and have not worn glasses for six years.

He was of the opinion that children are wrongly prescribed glasses and once labelled as having poor sight, these children could end up wearing spectacles for life. Leo says: "Children's eyesight is constantly changing and this depends on the tasks that they are performing and the state of their health, nutrition and tiredness.

Leo devised a means to spread and teach his message about his vision workshops. He called it Magic – Eyes workshops are sold in different countries.

The key idea here is that you need to realise a purpose that you want to invest in. You then endeavour to create a product or service to satisfy this niche and develop strategies to market and profit from the endeavour. The key idea here is the ability to know the idea that you want to bring to the market place and also develop the ability to sell and market your idea.

Thematically therefore you need to follow these steps to in the process of turning your passion into profit.

Step 1 You need to discover your purpose

This has been discussed in chapter 1. To recap you need to be clear and certain about what is you desire to accomplish.

Step 2 You need to develop your passion. Here the focus is that you strive to improve and become the best in that you love to do. The more competent you become the more will people be willing to use your product or service.

Here are seven steps, suggested by Kriston Thompson, that you can take to improve your level of expertise in your chosen field.

1. Choose a subject that aligns with your purpose

2. Study existing industry experts

3. Gain a meaningful degree of knowledge

4. Identify your niche

5. Position yourself to be highly visible

6. Declare yourself an expert

7. Become a creator

Step. 3 Create a product

This is a product that will solve your potential client's problem (s). It has to be a product of great value. You have to be able to package the product in a form that is implementable – text, audio, and video as the case may be. The format should be a form that is preferable to your consumer learning style.

Step. 4 You market your product for profit

The idea here is that you need a point of sale for your product. This requires that you become very knowledgeable in sales, advertising and marketing of your products. Remember my key point in this conversation is when the idea creator meets with an idea seller you are in a position to make your own good fortune. Becoming more proficient in marketing is the key to your profitability in business. In crafting the sales and marketing blueprint or plan you need to become fluent with the ability to creates, package and distribute your information product or knowledge to products that are of value to your prospects. This will enable you to develop different forms of offerings of your programs in a form that they can be monetised. Below are some of ways you can offer your programs to your prospects:

FREE LEAD CAPTURE	FRONT-END OFFERING	BACK-END OFFERING
• Special Report	• E-Book	• Membership Site
• Email Newsletter	• Training Manual	• Online Tools
• White Paper	• Worksheets	• Video Series
• Video Introduction	• How-To Video	• Training Kit
• First "Chapter"	• Podcast Series	• Webinar Series
• Podcast Interview	• Paid Newsletter	• Training Manual
• Basic Membership	• Exclusive Forum	• Exclusive Forum
• Interview Transcript	• Webinar	• Coaching Courses
• Facts Sheet	• Tele-Seminar	• Workbooks
• Research Findings	• Membership Level	• Combo Packages
• Article Directory	• Article Archive	• Done-for-You Kits

Source: Clickbank.com

These there prong steps or strategies consist of marketing and sales strategies to consistently and continuously keep abreast of the need of your prospects and keep them coming back.

The above there steps are ways to tap into your income stream as an information marketer.

Free Lead Capture

The free lead capture enables you to use any one of these information packages to urge your prospects to enter their personal information into your opt in or squeeze page.

Front end offering

These are information products that are fairly cheap that your prospects can buy into to become your customers. They are affordable and will definitely move them forward to solving their problems.

Back end offering

These are rather more expensive or products of higher value that enable your customers to do more – become more, do more and achieve more.

You can also become more creative and imaginative by transforming these information products into diverse income streams through leveraging their perceived value. For example, they can be transformed into Active, Leveraged, Passive and Recurring income streams. Your ability to do these depends on your imagination. The key principle here is to diversify your income/revenue streams which do rely on your time or your client. Essentially, how can you use technology to facilitate your delivery of your service with minimum contact for maximum implementation by your customer?

You have to raise your focus, hire a virtual assistant and productize yourself or leverage your product or program (turn your expertise, knowledge and ideas into content.)

CHAPTER 21

CONCLUSIONS – wrapping up!

The idea for taking you on this journey of turning your passion into profit is to help you hone the set of skills, attitudes and knowledge you need to make money with your chosen passion.

I have put together the set of knowledge base that you require to move from where you are at the present moment to where you desire to be in the bid to making your own good fortune. The important thing in this experience is the development of set of new abilities which are the outcome of the new experience. Knowledge you must have discovered is not enough, but you need to take action so as to achieve the result that you desire.

You have to be willing to change and adopt the model of change namely:

- Motivation (wanting to change) – the belief that the goal is achievable
- Means (knowing how to) – the knowledge of the physical and mental steps necessary to achieve the goal.
- Opportunity (having the chance to) – the necessary support and tools necessary to deal effectively with interference and resistance.

On the whole you have to develop the attitude of persistence the you can create the life you desire, that every goal is achievable, that every destination is navigate able (made of step from A to B), that I can harness both internal and external resources to create a path to get there and I can model the experience of others; and that if they can do it I also can do it.

I have to leave you with this insight, remember that at the back of all this demand for new and better things, there is one quality you must possess to win, and that is DEFINITENESS OF PURPOSE, and the knowledge of one you want, and the DESIRE TO possess it.

You also need a plan of action towards the accomplishment of your desire.

Remember the words of George Sheehan, "success means having the courage, the determination, and the will to become the person you were meant to be."

Therefore, follow your passion but remember to:

Watch your thoughts,

They become words.

Watch your words,

They become actions.

Watch your actions,

They become habits.

Watch your habits,

They become your character.

Watch your character,

It becomes your destiny....:

About the author

Benjamin is an avid reader, long life learner in the field of personal development as well as a writer. He writes in the Hubpages.com and you can read his articles at:

http://lemmyc.hubpages.com/

He is the Founder of Progress Path – Mastery Education a learning organisation dedicated to enabling people, grow and contribute to the society through teaching specialist knowledge.

You can find the website through this link:

http://progresspath-masteryeducation.com

He has his background in science and education and has motivated himself to acquire special knowledge in the fields of management, psychology as well as sales and marketing. His passion is to enable people realise their potential and this is the motivation for putting this work together.

He was a Rotary Ambassadorial Scholar and British Council Study Fellow; and an alumnus of University of Leeds and Leeds Metropolitan University both in the United Kingdom. He has a Certificate in Personal Coaching from the Coaching Academy, UK.

Ben is a born again Christian and worships at Bridge Community Church in Leeds; where he lives; and is happily married with three children.

You can access other resources by Ben in the www. Scribd.com – a digital library through this link:

http://www.scribd.com/ben_ugoji

I'll like to connect with you the reader to learn how this book has affected you.

You can contact Ben through his email at: bscugoji@execs.com

www.ingramcontent.com/pod-product-compliance
Lightning Source LLC
Chambersburg PA
CBHW020917180526
45163CB00007B/2773